Cage and Aviary Series

THE BORDER CANARY

Variegated yellow hen

THE
BORDER
CANARY

by

JOE BRACEGIRDLE

Past President: British Border Fancy Canary Club
International Judge of Border Canaries

**With Colour illustrations by
Michael Stringer**

SAIGA PUBLISHING CO. LTD.,
1 Royal Parade, Hindhead, Surrey
GU26 6TD, England.

Typeset by Inforum Ltd., Portsmouth.
Printed and bound in Great Britain
at The Pitman Press, Bath

SAIGA PUBLISHING CO. LTD.
1 Royal Parade, Hindhead, Surrey
GU26 6TD, England.

AUTHOR'S PREFACE

I first started to keep and breed Border Canaries in May, 1935, and have continued to do so every year since then except for the period of September, 1939 to November 1945 when I served in the Army during the war. I have been a Border panel judge since 1958, and have judged Borders at all the leading 'All Border Shows' in the U.K., including three times as a judge at the annual 'All Border International Contest Shows' held each year by England, Scotland and Wales.

I have judged Borders at the 'National Exhibition of Cage Birds' held at Alexandra Palace, London, which is the largest show of Cage Birds anywhere in the world. I have also judged Borders in England, Wales, Scotland, Eire, Spain in 1978 and 1979, Malaysia, and Australia in 1978 and 1980.

The breeding of canaries is not only a very relaxing and satisfying hobby, but it is also a wonderful way of making friends from all walks of life. During my 46 years of canary breeding there is just one thing that has always puzzled me and that is, why is it that so few ladies actively partake in this absorbing hobby? During my two visits to Australia I was delighted to meet many very knowledgeable lady canary fanciers.

For 27 years I was a Committee Member, Vice Chairman, Chairman and twice President of the **British Border Fancy Canary Club,** which is the only Canary Specialist Society to have:
1. Given £1,000 in awards at a single show
2. Received an entry of 2,196 Borders at a Show.

I would like to thank Roy Scott of New South Wales, Australia, Les Lockey of Cheadle, Cheshire for photographs, Bill Chilton of Cheadle, Cheshire, for their assistance, and my many fancier friends both past and present who, during the long years, have so willingly imparted their knowledge to me, and which has helped me to write this book.

Cheadle
Cheshire
September 1980   Joe Bracegirdle

v

Contents

Chapter		Page
	Author's Preface	v
	Monochrome Illustrations	vii
	Coloured Plates	ix
1	What Makes a Good Border	1
2	Care, Training and Showing of Borders for Novices	19
3	Canary Diet	31
4	Moulting Time	45
5	Winter-Time Management	53
6	Preparing for the Breeding Season	61
7	Disappointments During the Breeding Season	73
8	Tips for Novice Breeders	81
9	Exhibiting your Canaries	89
10	How Colour is Produced	99
11	Canary Management – January to December	107
12	Tips for Border Fanciers	115
13	Ailments and Corrective Treatment	121
14	Feeding and Food Values	125
Appendix		
I	Borders in Australia	131
II	Borders in Spain	137
	Index	143

MONOCHROME ILLUSTRATIONS

Figure   *Page*

Frontispiece Border Fancy Canaries: clear and evenly
marked.   x
1.1 The Border Canary – illustrating the British standard,
which is also adopted in Australia.   5
1.2 The Border Canary – illustrating the slimmer bird of
the American standard, which is similar to that of New
Zealand.   13
2.1 Main regions of a Border Canary.   21
2.2 Introducing current year canaries to show cages.   22
2.3 A little greenfood will encourage the youngsters to
enter.   22
2.4 A Dewar show cage.   27
3.1 Sprouted seed.   30
3.2 Essential seeds: canary seed mixed with red and black
rape seed; plain canary seed; hemp seed.   30
3.3 Useful wild seeds:
A. Persicaria
B. Plantain.   36
3.4 Valuable wild plants:
A. Shepherds purse
B. Seeding dock.   38
4.1 Treble breeding cages suitable for housing moulting
birds.   44
4.2 The author and his birdroom.   48
5.1 A garden birdroom (taken from an old book).   52
5.2 Double breeding cage built by Bill Chiltern.   56
6.1 Fawn and white hen with typical drinker attached to
her cage.   60
6.2 Wing of a bird partially stripped to show the insertion

	of the quills: feather patterns are all-important in breeding.	60
6.3	Canary nest pans of various types.	66
7.1	Hospital cage.	72
7.2	Plastic bird bath: a daily bath should be given, especially during the breeding season.	72
7.3	Numbered egg drawer.	78
8.1	Perching arrangements: A. Attaching the perch. B. Bird gripping correctly on suitably shaped dowel perching.	82
8.2	Typical canary nest pan, with rim for bird to grip on to.	82
8.3	Adult variegated yellow hen.	85
8.4	Unflighted variegated yellow hen.	85
9.1	How to handle a show cage while judging: A. Correct method B. Incorrect method.	88
9.2	Four basic stages in handwashing a bird: A. Correct way to hold a bird B. Dipping a bird into water C. Lifting bird from water D. Drying bird.	92
9.3	Equipment needed for hand washing Borders.	93
9.4	Six compartment Dewar show cage carrying case.	93
9.5	Extract from show schedule.	97
10.1	A Green Border (taken from an old book).	102
11.1	Nursery Cage, a useful item for the breeding season.	106
11.2	Natural foods of benefit to canaries: A. Watercress B. Seeding chickweed.	110
12.1	Birdrooms: the author's brick-built room, and a typical home-made breeding room.	114
13.1	Some effective remedies which the Border fancier should keep.	120
14.1	Useful feeding equipment: A. Multi-purpose plastic food or water container B. Clip on drinker.	126
14.2	The correct way to hold a canary for examination, to check condition, excess fat etc.	126
AI.1	Typical Australian canary room and flights.	130
AI.2	Framed Diploma awarded by the Border Canary Club of Victoria.	136

AII.1 The entrance point to the Barcelona Canary Show.   138
AII.2 A Spanish all-wire flight cage.   138
AII.3 Section in a typical Spanish balcony birdroom with all-wire breeding cages.   140

COLOURED PLATES

Plate
1   Frontispiece   *facing* Title Page
2   Borders in colour I   *facing* Page 98
3   Borders in colour II   *facing* Page 99

Frontispiece: Border Fancy Canaries: clear and evenly marked. This old print indicates the extent to which selective breeding has developed the shape of today's border. Compare with figure 1.1.

CHAPTER 1

What Makes a Good Border

EARLY DEVELOPMENT

This book is directed at those who wish to breed canaries as a hobby and have as yet not settled on any one particular variety. I suggest that they start with **Borders** for reasons which I give below.

It is a matter of historic significance that the Border has remained the most popular exhibition canary for a century. The Border Fancy originated in the 1850–1870s in the county of Cumberland* (now Cumbria). It was known at that time as the **Cumberland Fancy** and during the next fifty years or so its popularity gradually spread to the northern counties of England and over the border into Scotland. The Border became the most popular canary in Scotland and the north of England and this is why it was given its popular name.

A special meeting of Border breeders was held in Carlisle in 1890, and as a result of this gathering there came into being what we now know as the **Border Fancy Canary Club**. It was the first all-Border club to be formed in Britain, or for that matter anywhere else.

TOP OF THE POLL

Not only has the variety maintained its position at the top of the popularity poll, but it is still increasing in popularity. Evidence of this is quite clear; at leading shows there are almost as many Borders as all other varieties put together. The record stands at well over 2,000 Borders for a single show. Other breeds rarely achieve 1,000 entries.

Reasons for Popularity

A variety does not hold its position at the head of the Canary Fancy for so long without good reasons. So why has the Border achieved such universal appeal? The reasons are:

* **The exact origins are open to debate, a number of writers stating that the** Common Canary **originated in Scotland. However, the Border known today came from Cumbria.**

1. Relatively cheap to purchase

For a start, it is not the most expensive of canaries. Some varieties today may cost £100 or more. As this is mainly a working man's hobby, such prices, to me, are ridiculous. Quite good Borders can be bought for between £10 and £12 each. If you are just starting up, some fanciers may let you have birds for even less. So if you go about it the right way, stock birds can be bought at reasonable prices and you have every chance of breeding specimens which are good enough to exhibit.

2. Free Breeders

Borders are, in the main, free breeders and usually present few complications to the beginner. **Always pair a Yellow feathered bird to one of Buff feathering.** As Border Canary fanciers have always kept to this important rule, the variety has remained free from major feather faults.

By this I mean the birds do not have feather cysts, as is the case of some Norwich and Gloster Canaries, where in years gone by a great deal of Buff x Buff matings went on for countless generations.

3. Excellent Feather Quality

It is also one of the main reasons why Borders have been kept free from rough and coarse feathering. The quality of feather is of supreme importance in an exhibition Border, especially when the judge gets down to selecting his 'specials' winners.

Indeed, the *standard* of excellence for Borders is headed in a somewhat imperious fashion by a sentence which says that **a Border Fancy Canary of type and quality without feather quality is useless.** If we had to rely on two virtues alone — cheap to buy and easy to breed — the Border would be ideal to start with, but upon gaining experience the breeder could, of course, desert it for something more attractive.

That does not happen because this extremely nice bird has a charm capable of thrilling the most skilful breeders. Borders thus became a life-long hobby of many people.

4. Present A Challenge

The views of Border Canary fanciers differ on the pictorial ideal because it is only an outline drawing. Breeders have to form their own interpretation of an actual bird, but varying views should not make any difference to the success of the variety.

2

It is a matter of personal opinion and, perhaps, modifying the model a little from time to time. In so doing, both fanciers and the Border benefit and the variety marches on merrily from strength to strength.

Once a breeder becomes involved, he or she soon learns that there is more to a Border than the profile of a static bird.

I often think that a Border in a show cage is like a very skilled fashion model. Perfect in its movement, it is a bird with great appeal to the eye. I have heard visitors at a show, who were not fanciers, remark how attractively the birds stood and moved on the perches.

EARLY EXPERIENCES

Although I first started with Borders in 1935, my interest today is certainly far greater than ever and I would not part with my birds for anything. My birds keep me mentally occupied and by allowing me to meet other fanciers I retain an interest in the many facets of the Bird Fancy. The always-interesting Borders make me forget myself and think about them, the occupants of my birdroom.

Finally, a word to all those taking up canary breeding for the first time, who begin with a couple of birds and at the end of their first breeding season have only managed to breed a youngster or two. Strange to relate, in 1935 I set out with two pairs of Borders and at the end of that breeding season I had just one youngster. But I was delighted; I had done it on my own. I learned a lot and derived great pleasure from that modest start.

THE MOST POPULAR CANARY IS PUT UNDER THE MICROSCOPE

Britain

The British *Standard* of excellence and outline drawing of the Border have been accepted by almost every Border specialist society in the world. There is, however, one exception. That is the Fancy in New Zealand, where the standard calls for a much slimmer and shorter Border than we exhibit here: you could describe the Borders out there as similar to our Borders of fifty years ago.

United States

In the United States of America there are many former British and Irish fanciers who kept Borders in their homelands in their youth and

THE BORDER CANARY

STANDARD OF EXCELLENCE

The grand essentials of a Border Fancy Canary are TYPE and QUALITY, without these it is useless.

The general appearance is that of a clean-cut, lightly-made, compact, proportionable, close feathered canary, showing no tendency to heaviness, roughness or dullness, but giving the impression of fine quality and symmetry throughout.

Points		Points 'A'
10	HEAD – Small, round and neat looking, beak fine, eyes central to roundness of head and body.	10
15	BODY – Back well filled and nicely rounded, running in almost a straight line from the gentle rise over the shoulders to the point of the tail. Chest also nicely rounded, but neither heavy nor prominent, the line gradually tapering to the vent.	15
10	WINGS – Compact and carried close to the body, just meeting at the tips, at a little lower than the root of the tail.	10
5	LEGS – Of medium length, showing little thigh, fine and in harmony with the other points, yet corresponding.	5
10	PLUMAGE – Close, firm, fine in quality, presenting a smooth, glossy, silken appearance, free from frill or roughness.	5
5	TAIL – Close packed and narrow, being nicely rounded and filled in at the root.	5
15	POSITION – Semi-erect, standing at an angle of 60 degrees. CARRIAGE – Gay, jaunty, with full poise of the head.	5
15	COLOUR – Rich, soft and pure, as level in tint as possible throughout, but extreme depth and hardness, such as colour feeding gives, are DEBARRED.	25
10	HEALTH – Condition and cleanliness shall have due weight.	5
5	SIZE – But not to exceed 5½ inches in length.	5
100		100

Points 'A' are for Greens, Cinnamons and Whites.

1.1   *The Border Canary — illustrating the British* standard, *which is also adopted in Australia.*

took birds with them when they emigrated. This applies particularly to New York and adjacent states. In New York State, the Border *Standard* of excellence is similar to ours, but their birds do not exceed five inches (12.7 cm) and are correspondingly smaller in the body.

Australia

In Australia, especially in the states of Victoria and South Australia, the British *Standard* is followed closely. There they adhere to the real essentials of a Border Fancy Canary — **type** and **quality**.

Type

The main difference between breeds of canaries is the **outline**, or **type**. It is the type that makes the breed; and colour the variety. So it follows that type is the first requirement. If the bird is not a Border type, then irrespective of size or colour, it is not a Border.

Quality is that overall finish which cannot fail to attract attention. An otherwise almost perfect bird lacking quality appears to be unfinished and second-rate. What a pity some fanciers fail to realise that the appearance of a Border **should be a clean-cut, lightly-made, compact, well proportioned, sprightly and close-feathered — a smallest-size canary showing no tendency to roughness or dullness of feather.** It is a bird, in fact, which gives the impression of fine quality and symmetry throughout.

Clean Cut

The following points are important: clean cut, free from hollows or roughness to spoil the bird's smooth outline. Some careless interpretations of this are taken to indicate a bird on the skinny side.

Lightly-made

The term is 'lightly-made' not 'very lightly'. Our bird should be neither plump nor thin, but lightly-made irrespective of length.

Compact

Compact does not mean short and thick, but rather all of a piece. Well proportioned means that each part of the bird is in proportion to the rest.

Size

It is useless for one part to be the correct shape if the size is out of proportion to the rest of the bird. In other words, the head must not be too small or too big for the body, nor the tail too long or short.

Sprightly

Sprightly means an active, lively bird, hopping jauntily from perch to perch. This is impossible unless the bird is in tip-top health.

Close Feathered

Close-feathered means that every feather should be present, but not individually visible. The impression should be of a bird moulded in one piece.

Smallest-size

The Australian bird is described as the 'smallest-size' canary, that is to say, smallest compared with a Norwich or a Yorkshire. But it is not a small canary in the diminutive sense, as some would have you believe.

Quality

Showing no tendency to heaviness, roughness or dullness is obviously just another way of stressing the need for fine quality and symmetry throughout. In other words, the birds should have a beautiful finish.

Scale of Points

Scale of points adopted in the United Kingdom are:
head, 10; body, 15; wings, 10; legs, 5; size, 5; plumage, 10; tail, 5; colour, 15; position, 15; health, 10.

Australian standard points for excellence are:
head, 10; wings, 10; body, 15; legs, 5; size, 5; plumage, 10; tail, 5; colour, 15; carriage, 15; health, 10. A total of 100.

The points table can only be used to judge birds without a major significant fault. On points alone, an otherwise good bird with half the tail missing, or a fish-tail or extremely scissored wings, might earn 90 or 95 points. But it must be disqualified. Otherwise, to cite an extreme case, a bird with no wings at all could gain 85–90 points on the points scale. A closer look at the *standard* is now possible.

EXAMINATION OF STANDARD

Head and Neck

The head must be small, round and neat-looking, and not much bigger than a marble on the standard bird. Some seem to think a golf ball is the size. It should be **round** from all angles, including the front, rising sharply off the beak and going over in a perfect half circle with the eye near the centre of the head. Head faults are as numerous as they are unsightly — examples are: lack of frontal rise; flat; no back skull (which gives the appearance of no neck). Some heads, which appear round from the side, when viewed from the front are flat or pinched at the eyes. The short cut of producing big Borders at the expense of type and quality has caused many birds to be benched with a broader, square, poor, Norwich-type of head. By no stretch of the imagination can they be described as small, round and neat-looking.

Neat-Looking Head

To be neat-looking, the head must also be free from brows or horns. A bird with a really bad head should not win in good company as it lacks one of the main features of the breed; but a good head on its own does not carry an otherwise poor bird. A true Border head is probably the hardest feature to produce, and I feel that judges and breeders should pay more attention to the *standard* required.

Beak

A desirable beak does not spoil the balance of the head; nevertheless, we should not endeavour to take this too far: in some breeds of pigeons the beak is too small to feed the young and fosters are necessary. In other words, the beak should be small and neat, but in proportion to the size of the head.

Eye

The eye should be bright and dark, placed near the centre of the round head. Changing the position of the eye alters the apparent shape of the head. Bright and dark eyes are also signs of the bird's condition.

Neck

The neck should be rather fine and in proportion to head and body. It is one of the many features of a Border where a fraction of an inch can make all the difference. If we take a copy of the *standard,* and vary the outline of the neck at front or back by $\frac{1}{16}$ inch (1.5mm), or shorten or lengthen the neck by an $\frac{1}{8}$ inch (3 mm), it will be found that the overall appearance is significantly altered; introduce a slight thickening, and the neck tends to disappear so that head and body become one.

A neck only slightly too long or fine causes the head to separate too much from the body. The neck must be proportioned, just right to allow that fine, free poise of the head which is such a feature of a true Border's carriage.

8

An otherwise perfect head can be spoilt by a faulty neck. The general tendency is to be too full behind or under the throat. These faults are often found together.

BODY AND WINGS

The *back* should be filled in well and nicely rounded, running in almost a straight line from a gentle rise over the shoulders to the tip of the tail. **Nicely-rounded** refers chiefly to the curve across and along the back: but the term **well-filled** indicates that there should be no hollowness.

The gentle rise over the shoulders should be just sufficient to show that there are shoulders; there is no mention of a hump like a camel. A high rounded back is an asset in a stock bird and much preferable to a hollow back in an exhibition bird; but it is not an exhibition feature and must be treated like any other fault.

Wings should be compact and carried close to the body, just meeting at the tips. Close wings look as if they are part of the body, not a separate unit sitting on top of it. Wing faults are numerous and unsightly: for example, there are crossed or scissored wings; dropped wings, sometimes affecting one wing, sometimes both.

We find wings that meet at the tips but are held off the body; wings that are too long; and also double-flighted wings, which is a feather as well as a wing fault. Long wings are possibly the result of a Yorkshire cross used to improve position.

A hollow back is a common fault. Many birds have the correct shoulder line, but flatten out too much before the tail. Faulty wing carriage accentuates this fault.

The bird's **chest** should also be nicely rounded, but not heavy or prominent. The line should gradually taper away to the vent. As in other features, we are warned against heaviness, which is usually in the lower chest or abdomen, and prominence, which is usually higher on the chest.

In the Border we desire neither the exaggerated curves of Marilyn Monroe nor the bulkiness of Cyril Smith.* The features of a good bird may emphasise roundness, but to introduce **bulk** is entirely foreign to the true Border. In cross section the body is also round, and thickest near the shoulders, about one third of the way down the bird. Place a 10p piece on the *standard* and you will find it is nearly as wide as the bird depicted. A Border is not as thick as many would have us believe.

* **For the overseas reader it should be noted that Cyril Smith is a Member of Parliament of great body size.**

The line gradually tapers away to the vent in one continuous sweep from beak to tail. Too many birds fail from the legs back, lacking the draw so essential in a good Border. The chest can be too fine, giving the bird an undesirable skinny look.

The bird we seek is neither too plump nor over-thin. If you favour a thickly built bird, then breed **Norwich** canaries. If you favour a long bird, breed **Yorkshires**. But do not spoil the beautiful balance of the Border by introducing features contrary to the *standard*.

Any bumps or hollows that destroy the desired clean-cut line should be avoided. Fatness, if not checked, can spoil a good bird. Hens are more prone to this than cocks.

Legs and Feet

Legs should be of medium length, showing little thigh, and be fine in harmony with the feet and other points. Shorten the legs, and the bird is down on the perch, lengthen them and it appears to be on stilts. It is all a matter of proportion.

Showing a little thigh means that there should be just enough to indicate that the legs are not sticks stuck into the body. But the bird must not look leggy. At one time the *standard* was little or no thigh; a little thigh is obviously an improved requirement.

The clean, thin legs and feet should be free from scales or any missing nails. Feet should be fine, strong enough to grip the perch and hold the bird in its desired position, but always in proportion to the rest of the bird.

A slippery hind claw spoils a bird's ability to hold its correct position on the perch and virtually disqualifies its bearer. Missing claws are not major faults but must count against the bird, particularly when judging specials.

Plumage

Next, let us consider plumage. It must be close, firm and fine, presenting a smooth, glossy, silky appearance and free from frills or roughness. It is not easy to produce.

However, when perfection is achieved, what a joy to see! Many birds have close, firm, hard feathers, but lack the smooth, glossy, silky appearance that is so desirable. True Border feather gives the bird the appearance of being moulded in one piece. **Fine feathers make fine birds, but only the finest of fine feathers make a Border.**

Too many Borders have 'browiness', chest or neck frills, a twist in the feathers behind the legs or hard or coarse feathering. Some faults are caused by the introduction of Norwich blood to obtain size, and some simply because the breeder either will not or cannot handle

Cinnamon blood. Without good feather, we lack the fine quality essential to the Border.

Size

Size should not exceed 5½ inches (14 cm). This, perhaps, is the most contentious aspect of the picture of a Border and the *standard* wording is not entirely helpful. The trouble caused by the five points for size makes one glad that size is not worth 10 or 15 points! The idea of no points at all for size might avoid a lot of our present troubles.

Measuring in the conventional way is difficult and involves handling the bird. Perhaps the best way to judge a bird's length and, for that matter type and condition as well, is a life size model of the standard, 5½ inches (14 cm) long, placed in the back of a show cage.

Allowances must be made for parallax errors, or a bird may be accepted as bigger than it really is. Another rough check is to use the fact that perch centres are 4 inches (10 cm) apart.

The Border is a bird of **type**; providing it be of true Border shape it is a Border whether it is 4 inches (10 cm) or 6 inches (15 cm) long. Many so-called big Borders are short and thick, more like a small Norwich, and usually lie across the perch.

No experienced judge expects Yellow hens to have the length and substance of Buff cocks, and he assesses the birds accordingly. If a judge attempted to have all winners of similar size, he would finish up with small cocks and big hens as well as a motley lot in regard to type and quality.

Our standard bird is drawn at 5¼ inches (14 cm) and there is no denying that a really good bird of this size displays the true features of the breed better than a much larger or a much smaller bird of equal type and quality.

Really big birds rarely possess excellent feather and lack the true Border action in the show cage; the midget looks insignificant. There are no points for being diminutive or gigantic, so why attempt to produce such sizes?

The big Border makes a stock bird, and, if true to type, is invaluable in the breeding team. The really small Border, in my opinion, is undesirable in the breeding room. The best place for it is the pet shop.

Some claim that birds over 5½ inches (14 cm) are not Borders. But would it not be ridiculous if we had to measure all the birds and reject an otherwise perfect bird bigger than 5½ inches (14 cm)? Size after all, is only worth five points and comes into consideration only when all other points are close. Personally, I give full points to a cock bird of about standard size and penalise anything obviously over- or under-

11

BRITISH AND U.S.A. STANDARDS COMPARED

POINTS

	AMERICAN		BRITISH
HEAD	10	–	10
BODY	15	–	15
CHEST	10	–	—
WINGS	10	–	10
LEGS	5	–	5
PLUMAGE	10	–	10
TAIL	5	–	5
POSITION AND CARRIAGE	10	–	15
COLOUR	10	–	15
SIZE (Not to exceed 5^1/$_2$ inches in length)	5	–	5
HEALTH	10	–	10

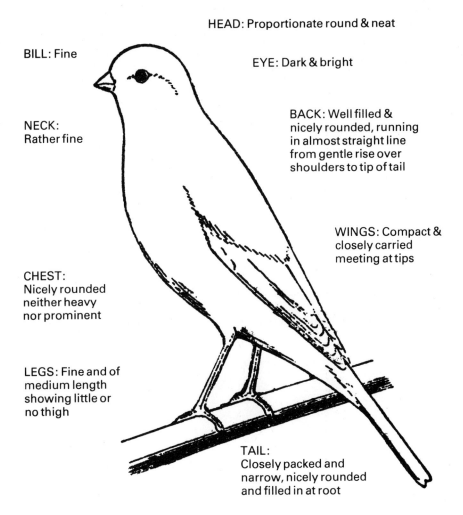

HEAD: Proportionate round & neat

BILL: Fine

EYE: Dark & bright

NECK:
Rather fine

BACK: Well filled &
nicely rounded, running
in almost straight line
from gentle rise over
shoulders to tip of tail

WINGS: Compact &
closely carried
meeting at tips

CHEST:
Nicely rounded
neither heavy
nor prominent

LEGS: Fine and of
medium length
showing little or
no thigh

TAIL:
Closely packed and
narrow, nicely rounded
and filled in at root

1.2   *The Border Canary — illustrating the slimmer bird of the American* standard,
      which is similar to that of New Zealand.

size accordingly. The extra-large or small specimens are as good as disqualified from the show bench. Allowance must be made for the fact that moulted adult birds are bigger than they were as unflighted young birds.

Tail

And now, the tail which is an important feature of the exhibition Border canary. When closely-packed and narrow, nicely rounded and filled in at the root it gains five points. Accurately described as a 'pipe tail', it is not even two feathers wide. A slightly spread tail is bad enough, but a fish tail ruins the bird's appearance.

It must be in line with the body, neither drooping nor rising up between the wings; either of these traits ruins the entire outline of the bird. The hinged tail is another Norwich heritage and if you are not careful it can be bred into the birds. Some tails, although not hinged, seem to curve downwards, giving the impression of a continuous curve from the shoulder to the tip of the tail as though the bird had been wrapped over a barrel; this completely spoils the balance.

A tail must be well-filled at the root to maintain the continuous sweep from underneath the beak to the tip of the tail. When a bird fails behind the legs, too much protrudes in front of the perch. A short tail gives the same impression; a long tail gives just the opposite. Both faults can spoil an otherwise nice bird.

Colour

Colour should be rich, soft and pure and as level in tint as possible. However, extreme depth or hardness, such as colour-feeding gives, is objectionable in this breed and should be discouraged. Birds must all be of a natural colour. There are 15 points for colour — something that is bred and not fed.

Richness should never be confused with depth of colour: one is soft and natural, the other hard and artificial. Level in tint means that the ideal is one even colour all over, richness without evenness gives a patchy appearance. A level but lighter shade is preferable. **Buffs** should possess the true mealy appearance so typical of the colour; they should not look like washed-out **Yellows.**

Dark markings on beak or legs of an otherwise **Clear** bird do not disqualify it, but count against the exhibit according to their extent.

Variegated birds should be the same rich ground colour as the **Clears**, but with bright green or cinnamon markings. The variegated parts are not usually as rich in colour as a **Self** bird. Nevertheless, the desired shade is pure green or cinammon — not the washed-out variegation too often seen.

The Green Border

Without taking colour into consideration the **Green Border** must conform to the *standard* on all other points. The correct colour should be a rich, level grass-green, and free from bronze or other tint.

Pencilling on the back should be clear, but neither broad nor heavy. Flank pencilling should be finer, but in harmony with that of the back.

Beak, legs and feet should be dark. Light beak, legs or feet are not a disqualification, but count against the bird according to the extent of the lightness. To be avoided are too dark a head; light patches under the throat or thighs; and lightness on the abdomen towards the vent or on the rump.

Young Greens carry a little bronze on the flight feathers and tail until after their second moult, but judges allow for this. Bronze colouring all over can be caused by too much **Cinnamon** blood, but I feel that the Cinnamon is often wrongly blamed, and some of the best coloured Greens carry a high percentage of Cinnamon blood. In fact, if it is correctly used, it is often the secret of good colour in Greens.

An olive colouring is due to the presence of too much ground colour; instead of being grass-green it is yellow-green. The object is to remove all the yellow, leaving the green and the black.

The ideal pencilling could be described as thin and dark. The thinner the pencilling, the more green is visible; the darker the pencilling, the more distinct it is. Too many birds have broad light pencilling.

Correct colour and pencilling are both necessary in a good Green Border. Many winning so-called Greens are not really Greens at all. While type must not be ignored, judges and breeders should pay more attention to the desired colour; it is, after all, worth 15 points. Buffs are naturally a different shade to Yellows, but a good rich Buff is still a Green.

The Self breeder has a harder task than the fancier producing Clear or Variegated birds. True colour is harder to produce in a Self than in a Clear or a Variegated, yet colour plus pencilling are still worth only the same 15 points as colour in a Clear.

One prominent judge maintains that only a reasonably coloured Green should be in the tickets. His argument is that bronze-coloured birds, not being Greens, are ineligible. Although this is a little hard, I must agree that with colour worth 15 points, a badly coloured bird would really need to be of very good type to beat an average bird of good colour: Ten to 15 points gives a bird a big lead.

The Cinnamon

The Cinnamon variety also conforms to the *standard* in all but colour. The colour has to be a rich, deep cinnamon tint throughout with faint markings on back and flanks. Greenish or too light thighs are to be avoided.

The main obstacle to good Cinnamon colour is not so much excess ground colour, that is, yellow, but excess green. The Cinnamon colour sometimes has a tinge of green right through it. This is due to insufficient thought having been given to the selection of pairs for breeding Cinnamons. The true Cinnamon colour is one of the hardest, if not the hardest, to produce to perfection in a bird of type: yet many breeders think they can do it with one or two pairs. The result may be either true type or colour; often it is neither, and seldom both.

The pencilling is of a darker cinnamon shade, not as distinct as in a Green, but it is still a necessary feature. Happily, the Cinnamon is becoming more popular with breeders, but some judges still seem biased against them.

White-ground birds

These were not in existence when the full written *standard* was first drawn up, but the following should serve as a guide to colour. The type is as for Normals and Clears and colour should be a pure white, free from any other shade. Many have a grey appearance instead of the clean, pure white look. Most carry a degree of yellow in the flights, particularly young birds, and some have this fault throughout the body colour: these are **Yellow White**. The exhibition bird is usually a **Buff White**. Although a bird is White-ground, it is still either Yellow or Buff. In the United Kingdom practically all Whites are Dominants, not Recessives.

Blues and Fawns

Next are the nice Blue and Fawn examples. The **Blue** should be rich blue, level throughout, and free from brown or yellow tints but with fine pencilling. It should also be free from the same negative points as a Green. The Yellow form, being richer in colour, is favoured as an exhibition bird.

Fawns should be a level fawn shade throughout, free from yellow with fine darker fawn pencilling, as with Cinnamons. The birds should be free from any light areas. The pale or Buff Fawn is preferred to the darker-coloured Yellow.

Colour-fed birds are barred, by mandatory ruling. To the experienced eye, a trace of colour-food can be discerned in a Border. Why

16

anyone should wish to colour-feed a Border is beyond me. Good natural colour is far nicer than the hardness of red-fed birds.

Position and Carriage

With regard to **position**, the bird should stand semi-erect at an angle of 60 degrees to the perch. The importance of these features should be obvious to all, for they share with colour and body the maximum rating of 15 points.

Semi-erect means neither too erect nor too low — higher than a Norwich but not as erect as a Yorkshire. Change of posture alters the outline of the bird, and thus its type. Perfect type can only be correctly displayed at the required semi-erect position. For this reason I feel that judges and breeders should pay more attention to this aspect.

A usual tendency is to lie across the perch at too low an angle, like the position of a Norwich Canary. This fault is particularly common among heavy-looking birds. These short dumpy birds, often hens, are very pleasant to look at, being level and round; in many instances they can win — but only due to the lack of opposition by birds of true Border type. Nevertheless, with proper matings, they can prove valuable stock birds.

It is rare to find a stance which is too erect, but it is still a show fault. Nevertheless, such birds are valuable in the breeding room to contribute to a strain of birds of good position.

The **carriage** should be gay and jaunty with a fine free poise of the head, and is worth 15 points. True Border action is beautiful to behold and the cock should move in a more graceful manner. Good health is essential for these features to be displayed.

The Border is a bird of movement, perfect type and quality. It loses some of the characteristics of the breed if it is what I call 'perch-bound'. The fine, free poise of the head is only present when the bird possesses a decent head and neck. Correct position and carriage must be bred into a bird, but most birds can be improved in position by training, and training probably also improves carriage.

Exhibiting

Many Borders work the back of the show cage, using only the back half of the perches, turning always from the judge. It is far more pleasing to see a Border move from perch to perch, hesitate, then turn towards the judge and jump on to the other perch before hesitating, turning away from the judge and repeating the cycle. In this way, a bird shows all possible aspects in each circuit of the cage.

17

An untrained Border can never be a credit to itself or the exhibitor. Judges certainly do not have the time to wait for it to show, and rightly pass it by. The winners are those that show at judging time, not on the Saturday afternoon when the show is nearly over.

A Border should move in one piece, without flapping its wings or moving the tail up and down. Condition and cleanliness also have due weight and are worth 10 points. Good condition depends on good health: a bird can be healthy, yet out of show condition; but a bird cannot be in good show condition unless it is in good health. **A bird out of condition should never be shown,** let alone allowed to win in good company.

Cleanliness of bird and cage are the only things over which the exhibitor has complete control. There is no excuse for losing a single point on these counts. A dirty bird or cage or an untrained bird are indications that the exhibitor is not really trying. Let your Borders earn the comment 'staged to win'.

We all differ slightly in interpretation and in weighting the relative importance of the various features and faults within the *standard*. That is only human. Trouble arises when people adopt a standard of their own, perhaps favouring a particular type which they, or their friends, keep. We may rate differently the importance of head against wing, or body against colour; however, we should all agree on the *standard* of perfection.

CHAPTER 2

Care, Training and Showing of Borders for Novices

Sometimes, a novice Border Canary exhibitor with a good bird is tempted to overshow it. This should not affect the bird adversely, **if it has been properly fed and conditioned**.

GENERAL CARE

Feeding

I noted during my trips to Australia that fanciers there give birds softfood throughout the year, especially when birds are returned to their cages the morning after a show. After the shows are finished, fanciers often give softfood or mixed seed on alternate days, together with whatever greenfood happens to be available. If greenfood is hard to come by, they substitute rape seed.

Sprouted seed is invaluable all the year round, especially during the breeding season. Here is a quick method of sprouting seed: soak the rape overnight for 12 hours; drain and wash the seed and spread it on a piece of damp hessian in a small tray approximately 12 inches (30 cm) square; cover with another layer of damp hessian. If this is kept damp, seed should soon show shoots a quarter of an inch (6 mm) long which can be used as required.

Bathing

Do not be frightened to provide baths all the year round at least two or three times a week, but put in the baths early in the morning and remove them by mid-morning. The only time the Australians withhold the bath is from the start of laying to incubation. Always be careful to hook up the door of the stock cage so that there is no chance of a bird being trapped in the water. This is a simple precaution that will save many regrets.

Young canaries should be allowed to bathe frequently. The bath

Main Regions (see Fig. 2.1)

1. Lower mandible
2. Upper mandible
3. Nostrils
4. Forehead
5. Crown
6. Superciliary region
7. Hind head, or occipital region
8. Ear, or ear feathers
9. Nape, or nucha
10. Back
11. Scapular wing coverts
12. Shoulder
13. Lower back, or tergum
14. Secondary quills, or secondaries
15. Tail feathers
16. Primary quills, or primaries
17. Vent
18. Belly
19. Wing coverts
20. Body, or lower breast
21. Shoulder margin
22. Breast
23. Throat
24. Chin
25. Tarsus, or leg
26. Front toes
27. Hind toe, or hallux

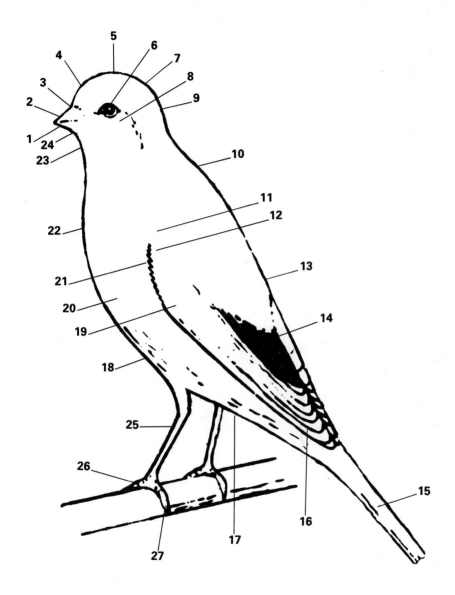

2.1   Main regions of a Border canary.

should be provided early in the morning and removed before noon, as it is important that the birds are dry by the time they go to roost.

MOULTING

Sometimes a bird may get 'stuck in the moult', in other words it starts to moult and then stops. This setback can be caused by a change in the weather, wrong environment or indifferent health.

Make sure that stock is **not subject to draughts or dampness** during this period, as both can interrupt the shedding of feathers. Should a bird be stuck in a moult, change its position in the birdroom: for example, if it is in a bottom tier cage, move it to one on top; if the bird is kept at one end of the room, switch it to the other end. **Changing position tends to start the moult.**

If this fails, place a few shreds of flowers of saffron in half a cup of boiling water. Allow the liquid to stand until cold, and give the infusion to the bird to drink. It should be prepared freshly each day. The bird should be placed in a quiet, dark corner of the room. Within a very short time the moult should recommence and the treatment can be discontinued.

The moult will usually progress until further interruption, but remember that the bird's **fitness must be maintained by providing it with a good, light, nutritious diet.**

During a bird's first moult from nest feather, it does not drop its tail or wing feathers. This is nature's way of assisting youngsters in the wild to escape from predators. In subsequent moults, all feathers are replaced, because by then the birds are wise enough to escape their natural enemies, even though they may be lacking a few flight feathers.

It can take up to thirteen weeks for canaries to complete a full moult. Even if they have apparently completed their change, do not stop giving them softfood, because there are still a number of small feathers to come through.

TRAINING FOR THE SHOW

Never show a bird that has just started to moult, or has not completely finished its moult; the change of plumage takes a lot out of it. A bird must be given time to get over this period before it is put on the show bench. In any case, an exhibit carrying pin feathers should never be among the winners.

We often hear fanciers say that a show bird is born and not made. This, no doubt, is true to a certain degree, though no matter how well

2.2   *Introducing current year canaries to show cages.*

2.3   *A little greenfood will encourage the youngsters to enter.*

a canary is bred, how good it is in type and quality and how perfect its markings, it will not win unless it has confidence in a show cage.

Introducing to the Show Cage

The initial introduction of current-year canaries to show cages should start early, so that the youngsters become used to them. Introduce young birds to the show cages when they are about four or five weeks old. At that time they should have sufficient confidence to look after themselves. To run a young bird from its quarters into a show cage is not always an easy task: canaries dislike enclosed places.

To begin with, fit a wire show cage to the front of the stock cage. This can be done quite easily by bending two pieces of wire to form hooks, which should be fixed to the top of the show cage so that it can be supported by the stock cage frame. Youngsters can then hop in and out at will. A little greenfood, such as a sprig of chickweed or seeding dock, placed in the show cage will encourage the youngsters to enter it and before long they become quite used to their new surroundings.

After the birds have been going in and out for a couple of days, carefully remove the show cage with the bird inside, making quite sure that the stock cage door is closed. Place it on a table or shelf in the birdroom and leave the bird in the cage for half an hour or so and carry on with your birdroom activities. Then run the bird back into the stock cage. This can be repeated for the next few days.

Although birds may have grown accustomed to show cages, placing them inside the **carrying case** may upset them, so this is another essential part of training.

Place the cages in a carrying case, close the lid and carry the case up and down the garden, indoors and out again. This is good training for the bird and will prevent it from becoming upset on its journey to a show.

Using Show Cage Drinkers

It is very necessary to train the young birds to use the show cage drinkers; to begin with, the normal drinker should be hung on the stock cage. When an old show cage is hung on the stock cage, make sure that it has a drinker full of water and also remove the drinker from the stock cage.

When familiarising the birds with the show cage, put between the wires of the show cages all the different kinds of greenfood and seeding grasses that can be obtained. Once a bird is trained to work or travel on the perches of a show cage it will always show itself off to its best advantage when exhibited.

24

Instilling Confidence

The next step in the training programme is lifting the cage containing the show bird to face level and, at the same time, talking to it. This will give it confidence. Do this 'drill' several times a day, and before long the youngsters will feel quite at home.

It is a good plan to arrange a row of show cages containing young birds to appraise them as a class. Some retain their required positions without any training, but occasionally a bird will lie across the perch instead of standing upright. Many fanciers place pieces of cardboard between the sides of show cages, so that birds are encouraged to look upwards to the required position in order to see the occupants of neighbouring cages. It is important to pay attention to the state of the perches. If they are too smooth a canary will become unsteady. It could then lose position and perhaps drop its wings or tail; on the other hand, it could develop a slipped claw. If the perches are roughened slightly the above defects can often be avoided.

Handle a cage in the manner of a judge, the idea being to get the bird accustomed to what is expected when it is on the show bench. Always handle the show cage with the greatest care, making sure that there are no sudden or unexpected movements. Offer the bird tit-bits to help to make it confident and steady.

First Shows

Young stock shows are good training grounds for canaries; they give them their first impression of a show hall. **Do not show them repeatedly:** once is quite enough. Always bear in mind that the birds are still babies, and **never show them too soon.**

Not every canary that wins specials at early events moults out to be an open show winner: the birds that do not pick up a ticket in young stock shows often moult out to become good open show winners.

FEEDING FOR GOOD BASIC COLOUR

Border Fancy Canaries must be bred for their natural colour and one cannot expect rich-coloured youngsters from parents that are pale. Nevertheless, careful feeding is important for good colour.

Some fanciers favouring natural coloured birds tend to discontinue the use of softfood when they see the chicks cracking and eating hard seed: this is wrong, for the gizzards and stomachs of the chicks are still tender. With that in mind, they should be given their ration of softfood right through the moult. It will help to keep them fit and will certainly prevent them from going light, which is nothing more than chronic indigestion.

Feeding During the Moult

During the moult, feeding can help to enhance the basic colour of our Borders. It should always be remembered that **the use of artificial red colouring agents or feeding that will give any unnatural colour is barred.** Nature herself provides the best food to increase the depth of the bird's natural colour. In the moulting period, natural food such as chickweed, thistle, shepherd's purse and seeding grasses, can be found in abundance in parks, allotments, gardens and open spaces. These can be collected and fed to the birds.

Some food can be gathered and stored for use later in the year, but make sure that the place from where it is gathered has not been sprayed with insecticide or weed killer as these preparations are deadly to birds.

Those who live in a city and do not have access to nature's larder can go to shops for greenfood such as lettuce, spinach, cabbage, brussels sprouts, chicory and watercress. The common marigold also has a place in the moulting cage; such food will enhance the natural ground colour of the bird.

Parrish's Chemical Food is a good tonic for canaries but if used continuously during the moult the birds will take on a distinctly pinkish hue, which can bar them on the show bench for being colour-fed. Play safe; a little will do no harm. Do not use it excessively every day and do not give it in a strong solution. It should also be noted that too much cod-liver oil fed during the moult tends to bleach a Border's plumage.

PRESENTING A GOOD SHOW BIRD

Steadiness is very important as far as the Border Canary is concerned, for not only has it to stand at the correct angle, which is 60 degrees to the perch, but also to appear jaunty in its movements.

In shows, more is required of the Border than other canaries. It must not only excel in natural colour, shape and stance; that is, wing quality, tail and legs, but also remain unruffled in strange surroundings and display itself to advantage before the judge in its all-wire cage.

Type and show quality are the result of good breeding, but **adequate training is still necessary** to make a good show performer. Nothing is more exasperating than to have a Border that looks excellent at home, only to find that it fails to show itself on the judge's bench. Many good birds are passed over owing to their inability to give their best at the right time.

Dimensions:
Length 12³/₁₆ inches (30.9cm) *Width* 4³/₄ inches (12.06cm)
Height 11 inches (27.9cm) at ends 9 inches (22.8cm)
Base ³/₃₂ inches (24mm) thick
Bottom rail 1³/₈ inches (3.5cm) by ³/₁₆ inch (47mm)
Corner posts 3¹/₄ inches (8.25cm) by ³/₁₆ inch (47mm) square
Drawer front 1¹/₂ inches (3.8cm) by ³/₄ inch (1.9cm)
Handle ¹/₂ inch (1.27cm) round head screw
Drinking hole ⁷/₈ inch (2.2cm) by ³/₄ inch (1.9cm)
Crossbar 4¹/₂ inches (11.4cm) from base
Frame 16 gauge wire; *Filling* 18 gauge wire
Finish to be black gloss

2.4   *A Dewar show cage.*

Between Border Canaries, more than other varieties, competition is very fierce: it is not unusual at our best shows to find classes of fifty to seventy birds. In this kind of competition, nothing should be left to chance. If a bird is good enough to bench, it is wrong to stage it badly; yet some fanciers are careless in their approach to showing.

The Cage

It may not be possible for everyone to stage their birds in absolutely new cages. In general, show cages are expected to last for years, but they need not be sent out in a shabby condition. I recently saw a good bird in a show cage that had cobwebs around it. The cage was probably being used for the first time after being stowed away at the end of the previous show season, but just five minutes work would have improved its appearance.

Many show cages are seen on the bench carrying old labels from former shows; I think this indicates carelessness on the part of the exhibitor.

Cages that have been painted time and time again should have the old paint removed and then be repainted. Those that are shabby need a fresh coat of paint.

Ensure that the perches are kept clean, for a Border Canary must have sound feet. The *standard* allows 15 points for carriage and position, and if a Border cannot use the perches properly, it is not going to gain points in this respect.

Caging birds together

It is inevitable that when several birds are kept together there will be playfulness as well as quarrelling and bickering, which can lead to the **loss of feathers**. A Border with missing feathers would have little chance of heading its class unless the competition was poor. This means that we must do our best to see that young birds do not lose feathers, because of the frolics of their companions.

In a cage of several young Borders, one is always more mischievous than the others. It is easy to pick out, because its feathers are usually in perfect order. Such a bird should be caged on its own, or with the adults, where it will soon be taught to behave itself.

A good show bird is spoiled by **sore feet or corns.** Young birds kept together seem to have an urge to peck at each other's feet; they will reach up and peck them if the perches are too near the cage floor. This can lead to injury, so position the perches to prevent it. It may not be possible to eliminate this annoying habit altogether, but we can ensure that the youngsters have plenty to occupy their minds.

Give seeding grasses to the birds to eat and to play with. A short piece of frayed, soft cord tied to the cage front will often keep a bird occupied for a long period. On no account allow the birds to become bored.

Assessing Potential

It is pleasing to see Borders that are approaching good show condition, and nothing gives greater pleasure than assessing their potential. It is true, however, that some birds which look unbeatable in the birdroom, never seem to give their best on the show bench. Conversely, of course, birds which lack brilliance in the birdroom can rise to the challenge of a show and return with the red ticket and sometimes even more.

Many good birds never win an award, often because the plumage lacks bloom or is a little rough in appearance. Such birds, mated correctly, could produce next year's champion.

A final piece of advice while on the subject of showing is to **exercise patience**. It is not wise to exhibit canaries before they are ready; very often, a week or two can make a great deal of difference to a bird's whole show future.

Comparison with other birds at the show makes the potential qualities of an exhibit easier to evaluate. If only the winners were entered, it would make a very poor show. A good show requires many good losers. It also needs generous club supporters, donors, hard working committee men and our wonderful ladies. They may be few but they are precious.

Rewards of Showing

Shows are the fancier's shop window where he can display his goods in competition with all-comers. Naturally, when he wishes to buy fresh stock he will select them from a strain of prize winners.

An exhibitor may not cover his expenses, his greatest compensation being the thrill and satisfaction he derives from winning, knowing his birds have been bred and managed to a high standard. Often many years of patient observation, feeding patterns, careful selection of stock and a gradual improvement in a strain become apparent on the day of the show. What a thrill a win can provide.

3.1   *Sprouted seed.*

Canary Mixture

Plain Canary

Hemp

3.2   *Essential seeds: canary seed mixed with red and black rape seed; plain canary seed; hemp seed.*

CHAPTER 3

Canary Diet

ESSENTIAL SEEDS

The following notes describe the nature and properties of various seeds used by most Canary breeders. They include commercial seeds, such as canary and rape, as well as wildfoods, such as shepherd's purse.

CANARY SEED

Canary seed is obtained from the seeding heads of the grass *Phalaris canariensis*. When fresh, good quality canary seed is opened, by removing the husk, the kernel inside will be found to be a rich, walnut brown colour; the outer shell of such seed is a pale gold colour, with a clean, bright appearance. Dull looking seed will always open up to show a very light- or a very dark-looking skin; this is a sign of bad harvesting or artificial drying. This particular type of seed is usually cheaper to buy, but in my opinion, is false economy, as the loss or illness of one good bird can make it far more expensive than the dearest of seeds. Cheapness and quality are seldom found together.

It is generally accepted by experts that large seed is best, but **size is not important as long as the seed is of good quality.** This seed is deficient in albumenoids (a substance found between the skin and the kernel of the seed) and fats by nearly ten per cent. At certain times of the year, this shortage must be made good by the use of seeds rich in these particular nutrients.

To sum up, one might say that canary seed is the basic foodstuff for canaries, and therefore one should be prepared to pay for the best canary seed, and to ensure that the seed supplied is the best. If in doubt, do not hesitate to query it with the supplier.

The analysis of canary seed is as follows:

water 13.5 per cent, **albumenoids** or **proteins** 13.5 per cent, **starch and other carbohydrates** 51.5 per cent, **fats and oils** 4.9 per cent, **ash and mineral matter** 2.1 per cent.

31

Rape Seed

This seed is one of the cabbage family, and is grown extensively in England and Germany. The leading authorities on seeds for use as bird food all generally agree that the **German summer rape** is by far the best.

It is a small reddish brown seed, with a rich, sweet, nutty taste. I always try chewing a little rape seed before I purchase it; if it tastes sweet and nutty then you can be assured that it is in an ideal state to give to your birds. Very often, in some areas, a wild turnip seed is sold but this is not particularly good for feeding birds.

A very **large black rape seed** is also available to us and is a fine quality seed, fed by many Roller fanciers. Many leading fanciers of my acquaintance use this rape practically all the year round mixed with various other seeds. From late January until the breeding season ends it is soaked and sprouted for use by the feeding hens during the breeding season.

Introducing Colour-food

Many fanciers use **crushed rape** as the basis of their mixed seed with which to introduce colour-food to their young birds. They crush the rape and then sprinkle it with their fingers over the mixed seed and blend it with a fork.

However, rape seed can, if used too freely, cause some trouble, by bringing that scourge of the birdroom — diarrhoea. Therefore, do not always leave the birds on this seed. Curiously, it does not always seem to affect all the birds, but seems to purge only one or two, and so I try to maintain a balance by limiting the proportion of rape to canary seed.

The analysis of rape seed is as follows:

water 11 per cent, **albumenoids** or **proteins** 19.4 per cent, **fats and oils** 40.5 per cent, **starches and other carbohydrates** 10.2 per cent, **ash and mineral matters** 3.9 per cent.

Thus the main nutritional content of rape seed is fats and oils.

Blue maw

Blue maw is produced from the poppy plant and is really poppy seed, since there is no maw plant. Contrary to popular opinion, maw seed contains no opium, which is derived from the flower and is not contained in the seed. This plant is usually acknowledged to have originated in Persia, but it is now grown in many parts of the world.

Maw seed is **in many respects the most valuable seed** available to the

Fancy. Some of us sprinkle it in the sand or shavings to teach young-sters to pick up during the final stages of weaning. It can also be scattered in the cages of elderly birds, as you will find that they spend more time on the floor of the cage than on the perch and pecking up the seed will keep them occupied, and contribute to their health.

No other seed is a corrective for both constipation and looseness of the bowels. I consider maw seed essential when preparing a mixture of condition seed. The oil in the maw seed is very nourishing, and is as palatable to the bird as best quality olive oil.

Maw seed is also of great help in curing youngsters of 'going light disease'. I emphasise this because many youngsters which have apparently gone light often make a complete and speedy recovery when fed on bread, soaked in milk and glucose and sprinkled liberally with maw seed.

The analysis of maw seed is as follows:

water 14.5 per cent, **albumenoids and proteins** 17.5 per cent, **fats and oils** 40 per cent, **starches and other carbohydrates** 12 per cent, **ash and mineral matter** 6 per cent.

Lettuce seed

Lettuce seed is rarely used by our aviculturists, but I consider it one of the finest seeds available. There are actually several kinds of lettuce seed, but the **white or light greyish type is the best** for use when fed to our canaries. The seed should be live seed. This can be checked by soaking it and watching it sprout; if it does not sprout it is old and of no use.

The seed has valuable tonic properties: it is very helpful during the breeding season; it has a definite purgative action and produces a cooling effect on the blood stream. It is also very helpful for reducing fatness without ill effects. It is very highly valued as a cure for wheeziness and voice troubles which occur occasionally in canaries. Lettuce seed is extremely **rich in iron** and thus is of great value in keeping the blood healthy. Among other things lettuce seed contains about 37 per cent potash, 7 per cent soda, 14 per cent lime and 6 per cent magnesia.

Gold of Pleasure

Gold of pleasure, or false flax, as it is sometimes called, is actually a member of the cabbage family, and has similar properties to charlock, rape, turnip and radish.

This seed is very oily, and has a very rich old gold colour when fully ripe. Its shape is small and round, and is only slightly larger than maw seed. As a food for canaries, it has much the same properties as shepherd's purse and is valued even more highly by some fanciers; one person I know says that gold of pleasure constitutes one of the secrets of some of the old timers who were such successful Canary breeders in years gone by. They claim that its use tightens and glosses the feathers in the late moulting stage and gives the feathers that all-important sheen and perfect finish.

This seed is claimed to be unrivalled at bringing hens into a successful breeding condition.

It contains much sulphur in a fairly assimilable state, which is of great medicinal value. Nevertheless, care should be taken not to over-feed this seed; do not return from a walk in the countryside laden with armfuls of it for the birds.

Teazle

The teazle that is harvested for sale by seed merchants these days is grown mostly in France although I have several fancier friends who grow it in their gardens quite successfully and harvest and feed it to their birds. The seed-head of the teazle plant, it is interesting to note, was at one time used in America to tease the cotton.

Teazle is extremely rich in assimilable nitrogenous matter, and is highly nourishing without containing the oily fats of some other seeds. It is a valuable food for canaries which are **showing signs of having over-fed on hemp or linseed.** Most experts claim it is essential in any mixture of condition seeds. If my supplier, because of his price, sends me condition seed without much teazle, I always add a little to the seed before feeding it to the birds. It is also very readily consumed by feeding hens when it has been soaked or is just beginning to sprout; before the war, my hens successfully reared young on nothing but soaked teazle, and bread and milk.

Niger

The plant producing this seed is a relation of the sunflower. Most of the world's supply of niger seed is grown in northern India and this is possibly one of the reasons why the price of it has increased greatly during the last few years. The local people grow it principally to produce lamp oil and good seed may yield as much as 40 per cent oil when crushed.

To be suitable for consumption by birds, niger should be jet black in colour, clean and **unbroken,** and very shiny. Niger is easily broken in transit because of its length; old and broken niger can be most harmful to birds, because the oil content of the seed becomes rancid.

Niger has a similar food value to hemp, for which it may be used as a substitute. Top quality seed fed to hen canaries during the winter months and very early breeding season is most beneficial. I scatter it on the floor of the flight cages containing the breeding hens during the winter months and I watch them spend hours picking up and eating the niger seed from the wood-shavings on the floor of the cage. This is exceptionally good for them; its rich oil content helps to prevent birds becoming egg-bound even in cold weather. I always include at the same time a handful of charcoal.

The analysis of niger seed is as follows:

water 8.5 per cent, **albumenoids and proteins** 17.5 per cent, **fats and oils** 33 per cent, **starches and carbohydrates** 15.5 per cent, **ash or mineral matter** 7 per cent.

Shepherd's Purse

Shepherd's purse is a garden weed of far greater use to the bird fancier than perhaps some people appreciate. In all stages of its growth it is perfectly safe to use even for very young birds that have just been weaned. Shepherd's purse is to be found growing wild in many parks or in previously cultivated soil which has been left since it was turned over, such as in spare allotments. It grows between six and eighteen inches (15–46 cm) in height and the seed is contained in purse-like pods in considerable numbers at the ends of each stalk or branch of the plant. Breeding hens will readily take these stems when they are ripe, or even half-ripe, and will extract the very tiny seeds which are white when partially ripe and very succulent.

Several other weeds resemble shepherd's purse but few, if any, produce seeds of comparable nutritional value. In addition, the birds so much enjoy eating it, that it should always be included in their diet.

Hemp

Hemp is grown extensively in America and southern Europe; it grows to quite a large tree about five or six feet (1.5 m – 1.8 m) tall. It produces both male and female flowers, and it is the female flower which will contain the seed. High quality seed varies from white to dark olive green in colour. Hemp of a light green colour is generally unripe; that of a very dark grey shade and very light in weight is old and useless.

This seed is very nourishing and can be fattening and warming; it is therefore **more of a winter seed** than an all-the-year-round one. Hemp is an excellent form of food for breeding Canaries; many breeders

*3.3   Useful wild seeds: A. Persicaria
B. Plantain.*

claim it to be almost essential during the nesting or breeding period. Some people crack the hemp seed, while others soak it until it just begins to sprout, and then supply it in limited quantities to the feeding hens.

The analysis of the seed is as follows:

water 12 per cent, **albumenoids or proteins** 16.5 per cent, **fats and solids** 32 per cent, **starch and other carbohydrates** 16 per cent, **ash or mineral** 4.3 per cent.

Linseed

Linseed comes from the common flax plant, which is harvested as an annual crop. This seed, or its large variety has been used by horse trainers and breeders for many years to produce that delightful sheen on the coat of horses, which is so great an asset at shows. Similarly, when fed to canaries in correct quantity, it helps to produce that sheen and lustre in feather which all true fanciers strive to achieve when the birds are in their moult.

As linseed's main effect is demulcent (soothing) it is particularly useful during the moult, as well as for promoting richness of feather. Good quality, fresh linseed is valuable to us as bird food; however, cheap, dirty, dusty and old seed can be most harmful; that is very important to remember. It may contain rancid oil which can seriously injure the bowels; feed only good, fresh linseed to your birds.

Linseed is claimed to contain over 100 grains of protein to an ounce. Fresh eggs and wheat contain only 60. It must therefore be realised that linseed is a highly concentrated form of food and should be used in moderation for success.

Soaked Linseed

Soaked linseed can be used to make a successful drinking water for birds: soak some linseed for 24 hours in cold water; strain off the liquid and add to it 50 per cent water. When birds are given daily fresh water which contains linseed water, it is important to clean the inside of the drinker to remove any deposits which could be potentially harmful to your birds.

Persicaria

Persicaria is another wild seed which is very good for birds, be they canaries, British birds or budgerigars. It can often be seen growing between rows of potatoes; its flowers are white, tinged with red. The seeds are much appreciated by birds when they are moulting.

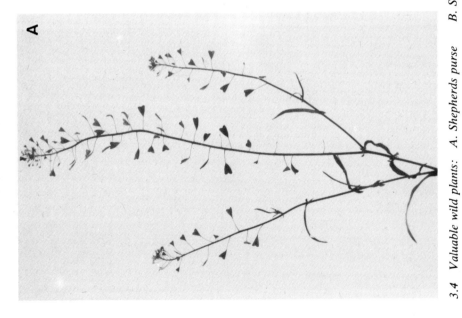

3.4   *Valuable wild plants: A. Shepherds purse   B. Seeding dock.*

WILD PLANTS AND THEIR FOOD VALUE

Like the majority of Border Canary fanciers, I am a firm believer in the use of various wild plants and seeds to keep my stock in its peak condition. Below, I discuss the main plants and food supplements which ensure the good health of young and adult birds alike. This is an extension of the coverage given in the preceding section.

Dandelion

The dandelion is unique amongst our native weeds.

There is hardly a finer tonic to be found in the countryside; it is rich in mineral salts, calcium, iron, magnesium, chlorine, sulphur and phosporus, and makes an excellent blood purifier. It is also used for stomach and liver disorders. Both seeds and roots are eaten as they have a tonic effect on the heart and spleen.

The fresh leaves have such a high food value that they can wholly replace greenfood such as sowthistle heads, spinach and other seeding heads when youngsters are being reared. Dandelion is fed extensively throughout Australia.

Juice crushed from the root of the dandelion can be given in water once a week. Crush half a pound of washed roots with a little water and then dilute the mixture up to one gallon. It should only be given for one day, as in warm weather it will begin to ferment.

Chickweed

Chickweed may be used with good results at any stage during its life, either the succulent seeds or fresh leaves.

The green leaves and shoots are rich in those chemical elements vital to good health and fitness and have a pronounced effect on the bloodstream. The mature plant is favoured by hens for their nestlings.

Dock Seed

Dock seed improves the plumage. It contains a large percentage of oily matter of a most wholesome kind making it a valuable autumn food for maintaining the bird's body temperature and preventing chills. The oils also serve as a fine internal lubricant, keeping the bowels in such a healthy condition that there is no morbid accumulation of fat and, therefore, this seed has been used to correct a tendency to excess weight.

Lettuce Seed

Lettuce is an extremely valuable item of diet for canaries. The suggestion sometimes heard that it contains an opiate is apparently false. Its value is not as a colouring agent, but as a source of minerals and abundant vitamins.

Maw

Maw is poppy seed; is readily digested, very nourishing and comforting and excellent for conditioning.

Plantain

There are two species of plantain; the one most commonly used is called rat's-tail. It is found in fields alongside streams and elsewhere near fresh water.

It is a highly nourishing and valuable medicinal food; the copper content ensures a strong and brilliant plumage after the moult.

Mustard Seed

The white variety is rich in proteins and fats and is very warming and stimulating. It should not be given in excessive amounts, particularly in warm weather.

Shepherd's Purse

This plant can be grown in the aviary without hesitation. The small seeds are of a 'hot' nature, nutritious, and stimulating to the stomach.

Teazle

Teazle is a natural and very nourishing tonic. It may be grown, with care, in the aviary.

FOOD SUPPLEMENTS

Natural Minerals

Sea sand is, without doubt, one of the finest forms of grit for all cage birds. Sand differs along various parts of the coast, but the best comprises about 50 per cent shell particles.

A frequent question is whether the sand should be washed before it is given to birds? The answer is **No.** If sand is washed with rain or fresh water, it loses some of its natural mineral salts, including iodine.

Sea salt is the most balanced form of salt for living tissue. The product sold for cooking and flavouring our food contains too much sodium salt and too little potassium salt. The latter, for our purpose, should always predominate.

The best sand to obtain is one which has been covered and exposed daily by the rise and fall of the tide. Constant drenching with sea water followed by drying in the sun, enriches the sand with numerous minerals, all of them beneficial. Sand removed from places above the water line has lost some of its mineral wealth.

The usual method is to collect sand at low tide and dry it out by placing it in the sun. Care should be taken to avoid collecting sand from polluted areas. Damp sand is best stored in wooden or PVC boxes, because metal rusts. The amount of grit taken depends on the amount of food eaten each day, because sand is consumed to grind the seed diet and render it digestible.

During the breeding and moulting seasons, an adult Canary's appetite for hard and soft food varies with the age of the nestlings to be reared, or the phase of the moult.

Egg, is rich in those ingredients which seed lacks, and makes an **excellent dietary supplement.** The protein and fat content of egg is similar to that of meat.

The organic phosphorus content of egg yolk is very high, and only milk has so much calcium. It is an ideal preventative for anaemia. White of egg is rich in albumen and contains large quantities of organic sulphur. The whole egg is an ideal food for growing birds.

Vitamins

It is probable that canaries suffer more often from lack of Vitamins A and D than the B and C vitamins. A considerable number of birds may hatch out, grow, reproduce and die without exposure to direct sunshine. Many Rollers are kept in dull light much of the time to keep their voices low and soft.

FOOD FOR SPECIAL NEEDS

The breeding season

In the breeding season the use of liver extract and vitamins in softfoods is recommended. I first learnt of the value of using these nutrients while on a lecture and judging trip to Australia. The particular fancier who recommended the use of liver extract successfully reared 310 young canaries from forty hens last season from only two rounds.

Pre-moult Care for a Winning Bird

In a class containing several quality birds, the **standard of feathering** is very important indeed, if a bird is to win its class. With regard to **feather colour**, it does not make any difference whether it is Yellow or Buff. No artificial colouring is permitted in Borders. All good breeders and exhibitors (including myself) supply their birds with food which will enhance the natural depth of feather colouring, before the start of the moult.

A Good Moult is Necessary

An important task is to get the young Canaries through a good moult for two reasons:

1. A quick, clean moult results in a bird producing good quality silk-like feathers, the colour of which I will discuss in due course.
2. It will be found that most Canaries which have a slow drawn out moult, develop coarse feathering which gives them a second rate appearance, no matter how well they conform to type.

In Australia and most European countries, it is no longer advised to feed **green cabbage leaves** to Borders or Glosters. On the other hand, fanciers who keep Colour Canaries in these countries will supply this food *ad lib*. I have now stopped feeding cabbage leaves during the moulting period.

Some Beneficial Foods

Some greenfoods and wild seeds, fed to Borders before the start of the moult, will prove beneficial:

1. **Young dandelion leaves,** with their high content of mineral salts, calcium, iron and phosphorus, will improve feather growth and help to purify the blood.
2. **Dandelion root,** when cut in half lengthwise to expose the sap inside, may also be used. The root sap tends to stain the plumage and so care should be taken to avoid its usage when the birds are moulting the facial feathers.
3. **Seeding spinach heads** and the succulent, green seeding **dock** are greatly enjoyed by the birds, the latter containing a large percentage of oil, which is helpful in maintaining feather growth and gives the plumage that extra sheen. When the dock seed turns dark brown in colour, it develops a very hard husk, which canaries find difficult to crack, but which most British Hardbills still enjoy.
4. **Linseed.** Two or three times a week I like to feed my moulting birds a little linseed, which helps provide a nice lustre to the birds' feathers.
5. **Plantain** is a very useful wild seed and one which keeps well in winter, stored in plastic bags. It contains copper which helps to ensure a rich, strong plumage.

6. **Shepherd's purse.** During the difficult weeks of the moult, it acts as a tonic and keeps the birds active and interested in their food.

7. **Sprouting teazle seed.** While expensive it represents good value, especially to all young birds having their first moult.

While advising against the use of nasturtium flowers to moulting birds, I do recommend the feeding of the green plant leaves, as they really give a depth of colour to the plumage, without distorting the actual colour of the feather.

For those who are able to obtain a ready supply of **clean, beach sand,** this is invaluable as a source of iodine. In Australia a large percentage of canary fanciers make liberal use of it in cages and covered outside flights.

Colour Stimulants to avoid

Colour stimulants should be avoided; examples are as follows:

1. Do not use **marigold or calendula** flowers, because when used with certain types of greenfood, they produce a Yellow or a Buff plumage with too much depth of colour, which mars the essential natural feather sheen.

2. The **nasturtium** should also be avoided — both the red flowers which some fanciers feed to their Yellow birds, and the yellow flowers which are given to Buff-feathered birds.

3. **Green cabbage** leaves.

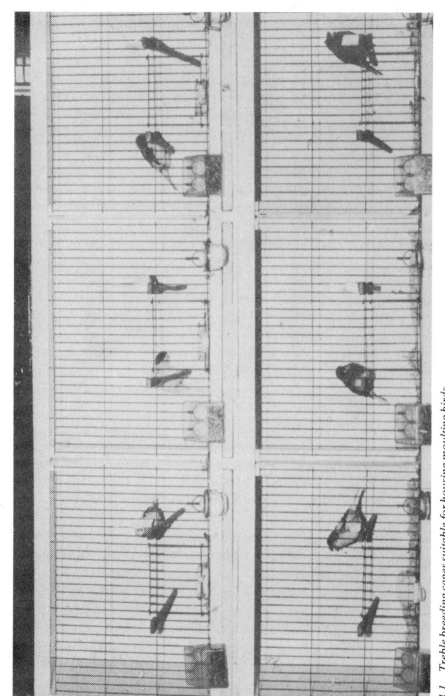

4.1 Treble breeding cages suitable for housing moulting birds.

CHAPTER 4

Moulting Time

SEE THAT THEY ENJOY A GOOD, QUICK MOULT

The most important target to aim for is a **quick, clean, healthy moult.** You will find that any canary which has a prolonged, lengthy moult has feathers which are coarse and poor in quality.

Just what can a breeder do to ensure that the desired results are achieved? There are many **do's** and **dont's** that I have learned over the years and here are just a few of them.

For the two months during which the birds are actually undergoing their moult, I ensure that they receive the minimum of handling and are disturbed as little as possible. I leave six or seven together in a treble-breeder with a perch at either end of the cage. During this time, no show cage is hung in front of the stock cage of moulting adult Borders.

A daily bath is essential, but **ensure that the water is not too deep.** I think that if a moulting canary has a thorough soaking each day, the bird's reserve of stamina may be reduced. The all-important rule is **'a little and often'.** This moisture can greatly help both the rate of growth of the feathers and their quality.

Another important factor which the breeder has to take into consideration is the colour of both Yellows and Buffs. I have learned from experience over the years that various greenfoods can have a definite effect on the final colour. A daily supply of fresh, young dandelion leaves is readily enjoyed by the birds and has a good effect on the plumage.

For those living in a city or large town, who do not have ready access to dandelion, there is a very good substitute — **watercress;** it contains not only iron but also Vitamin C which is equally good for the birds. The only criticism I have of watercress is that it can quickly go yellow unless precautions are taken. First, remove the elastic band from around the purchased bunch, then immerse the watercress in a bowl of cold water for about ten minutes; remove it and gently shake off the surplus water; place it in a plastic bag and roll it up so as to exclude the air from the greenfood. Finally, place the bundle in the bottom of a refrigerator where you will find that it will keep quite fresh and green, with no waste, for at least four days.

I am told by Les Gough, secretary of the **Border Fancy Canary Club of Victoria,** that in Australia they put handfuls of seeding grasses in the birds' cages at moulting time. They also feed the birds dandelion and as a result the stock has plenty of natural colour, as I have seen when judging out there.

In Spain, during the moult, Border breeders feed their birds on a mixture of two parts plain canary seed to one part black and red rape. They also supply a separate mixture of equal parts of teazle, linseed, hemp, clipped oats and niger seed — all served in small quantities daily.

They give their birds fresh water daily and five days in every month a vitamin solution is added to the water to the ratio of 5 cc to 1 litre of fresh water.

For softfood, most Spanish fanciers use one that is sold by seed merchants and add to it an equal part of ground soya beans. Wheat germ flakes are also added with a hardboiled egg which has been passed through a sieve. The mixture is stirred together without adding water.

For greenfood, my Spanish contacts who live in towns are totally dependent on local greengrocers for such items as lettuce, spinach, radish tops, carrots, plus, of course, fresh fruit when it is in season. I am told that in Spain the sickness **'going light',** as we refer to it, never occurs.

Separating birds with show potential

When the birds are three-quarters through the moult, I select those that are revealing show potential and put them two to a single breeding cage, and place a show cage on the front. After a fortnight, I carefully run these birds into other show cages for half an hour, and place them on my judging bench.

When they are settled down, I handle each cage and go over the birds thoroughly, looking for any faults in them. When I have satisfied myself as to their show potential, the pick of the bunch are housed on their own in single breeding cages.

Each day a bath of water is hung on the cage, preferably in the morning, and then when the birds have dried off fully I hang a Border show cage on the cage front. The show cage contains greenfood, such as plantain, green seeding dock, etc, or perhaps a small slice of apple pressed into the wires.

At this time, cleanliness of cages and perches is most important. I clean out the cages twice a week and put plenty of sawdust or fine wood shavings on the floors of both stock and show cages.

When handling the birds I make a point of picking up the show cage by getting hold of it by the top of the cage and not from the bottom or the wooden sides. There is a very good reason for accustoming the birds to being handled in this particular manner. When judging Borders in all parts of the United Kingdom, I have seen stewards carrying two show cages in each hand, with their fingers holding the wires at the top. Borders, which are not used to being handled in this way, are not at their best when they are judged, and that is why it is not until the second day of a show that all of the birds are nicely relaxed.

THE BIRDROOM

The birdroom affects the moulting process. My birdroom is brick-built; it has windows in two sides which face north and west. I was concerned at the amount of condensation and water which collected on these windows during the winter period, and as soon as possible, double-glazed the windows. It is surprising how much the condensation on the glass has been reduced and how few pools form on the window ledges.

Arrangement of Cages

On the right-hand wall is a single unit of twenty-five single breeding cages, each 18 inches (46 cm) wide, which by the removal of slides, can be made into double or even treble size cages. From experience I have found that 18-inch (46 cm) single cages are quite large enough for the Borders to breed in.

On the opposite wall there are twenty singlebreeders in a single unit. Both these two units of cages are mounted on castors and it is quite easy to pull them out when I want to apply emulsion paint to the walls behind.

Insulation

To the pitched roof I have fitted $1\frac{1}{4}$-inch (3 cm) thick insulation tiles, each of which contains a pattern of $\frac{1}{4}$-inch (6 mm) deep holes for decorative purposes, but they have provided most effective insulation and maintain an even temperature inside the birdroom during both the winter and summer months.

47

4.2   *The author and his birdroom.*

Housing the birds

During the months of January, February and March I run four or five hens into a treble-breeding cage, making sure that each cage contains plenty of cuttlefish bone. I also scatter on the floor a handful of charcoal; the birds' eagerness to peck at the charcoal clearly shows that they really enjoy it. I make a practice of tying up a large piece of butcher's suet in each cage at the end of a perch, and in a month or so all has been eaten up.

I put **one** cock in each singlebreeder. During the actual breeding season I only use the cocks to 'fill' the eggs. Once a pair has mated, I return the cock to his own cage for ten minutes and then I try him with another hen, and I get very few clear eggs. I have time to run the cocks in and out of the cage five or six times a day.

MOULTING PERIOD TESTING TIME FOR CANARIES' STAMINA

The moult may determine whether a canary comes in the first two in its class or becomes a section winner. The more quickly any canary completes its moult, the better will its condition be when the show season commences. I think that to some extent the end result is related directly to the kind of management before and during the moulting period.

Like anything else in life, the result depends to a large extent on the effort put into it.

Personally, I have always thought that the moulting period tests a canary's bodily fitness and reserves of strength. We can remove 70 per cent of the problems appertaining to the moult by consistent and good management.

Be sure to feed a **well balanced and varied diet.** I suggest the following procedure:

1. Feed only good quality **canary seed and rape** in the ratio of 4 parts canary to 1 part of rape.
2. Give the birds a little good quality **softfood**, such as one advertised in *Cage and Aviary Birds*. It should be offered twice a week to adults and four times a week to unflighted birds.
3. Supply a small amount of **bread and milk** with glucose added twice a week, making sure that it is not too milky.
4. I like to give young birds in their first moult a little **soaked seed** on most days; in the case of adult birds, I give soaked seed every other day.
5. It is very necessary to give the birds some form of **greenfood** every day such as dandelion, watercress, growing black rape leaves, plus, of course, shepherd's purse, seeding dock, plantain, or other wild food.

49

6. The **daily bath** must not be overlooked. You will find that most birds love to bathe and this is very beneficial both to feather growth and the quality of the feather. Do not offer a bath full of water; only leave about ¼–⅜ inches (6–9mm) of water in the bottom.

There are always a few birds which will not go into the baths which you have put on the cage fronts. For these particular birds I have a special old type show cage in which I have made a series of holes in the bottom left-hand corner through which the water can drain off. The birds are run into this particular cage and gently sprayed. The cage is held outside the birdroom to avoid the floor getting wet.

7. As the birds are all developing new feathers, **cleanliness** of perches and cages is something that should not be overlooked.

8. With unflighted birds some fanciers make a point of **drawing their tail feathers** during the moult. The idea is that should one of these young birds lose one or more of its tail feathers, the new feathers will all be the same length.

9. Hygiene is essential: all dishes containing softfood, bread and milk or soaked seed, drinkers and the interior of the stock cages should be kept spotlessly clean at all times.

While the birds are moulting I give them three drops of **Parrish's Chemical Food** in their drinkers twice a week (available from Messrs Thornton and Ross Ltd, Linthwaite, Huddersfield, Yorkshire).

In many cases special treatment for condition is required but it cannot be overemphasised that it all amounts to nothing without success in rearing and moulting. Many birds require no further treatment and those usually make the best exhibition birds. **First-rate show condition** implies perfect health and cleanliness and just enough flesh to give a finish to a bird's shape. Too much weight will mar the symmetry of the particular variety. Injured or misplaced plumage must be avoided, therefore a bird must be steady when in the show cage. It must show off well and not damage or disarrange its plumage.

Unflighted

For the beginner it should be explained that when canaries have their *first* moult they grow a complete set of feathers except for their wing and tail feathers; these are moulted out when the birds are 12 months old, which is why the term '**unflighted**' is used for a young bird. At the next moult these feathers are moulted out and new feathers grow about ¼ inch (6 mm) longer.

Rough-cut sawdust is useful for keeping the new feathers looking clean and fresh for as long as possible. I get a good supply and, when cleaning out the birds, fill a bucket two-thirds full of sawdust and make it damp by pouring a small quantity of water on the sawdust and stirring it up by hand.

While the young birds are moulting, I cage four to a double breeder and hang on the front an old show cage with perches made from twigs.

When the birds are three quarters of the way through the moult I pick out those that look to be most promising for type and colour and put them in twos in single breeding cages. Several times a week I run these birds into separate show cages and place them, six show cages at a time, in a row on the window ledge.

The Young Bird in Peak Condition

Year-old birds that have had their second moult or their first full moult (including moulting the wing and tail feathers) **are regarded as being at their very best.** While they moult out as cleanly as those that are a season younger, they are more finished in plumage, having obtained their second flight and tail feathers with the richer tint of colour. This gives a finish not possessed by young birds.

The skin of the legs and toes of a young bird is very fine in texture; it has a more tender and fleshy appearance than that of a yearling or even older bird which has a more horny surface, almost a scaly roughness, especially on the top of the toes.

The toenails of a young bird are also much finer and a brighter flesh colour than those of an old bird. The vein down the centre (called the quick) comes further down the nail of a young bird than in an old one.

There are exceptions, however, and some old birds cover their age with such juvenile smartness and finish that they puzzle the best of judges. On the other hand, some youngsters very quickly develop marks of age. In estimating age, it is necessary to exercise caution and, above all, to take into consideration the bird's health, which can materially alter the appearance of the legs.

5.1   A garden birdroom.

CHAPTER 5

Winter-Time Management

PERIOD OF PREPARATION

The winter-time of the year is regarded by some fanciers as a waiting period between the end of the show season and the commencement of the breeding season at the end of March. It should be a very important time of the year, spent preparing birds for the coming breeding season.

The months of January and February often decide whether you will have a good or an indifferent breeding season and during this period, time should be spent in the birdroom to pay particular attention to the hens. It is very important that they are correctly conditioned; a bath is hung on the front of their cage every other day; softfood is fed three times a week; and twice a week **Parrish's chemical food is put in their drinking water.**

The hens are normally kept five to each treble breeder and the cocks placed in single breeding cages. Last year, I kept fourteen hens and six cocks to breed from; two of the latter were paired up to four different hens in the first round.

Balanced Diet

At this time of year try of give the birds a fully balanced diet. Besides softfood, they should have condition seed twice a week and some form of greenfood every day, such as watercress or the outer leaves of sprouts. Make a point of giving the hens a little bread and milk twice a week. Not only is this good for them, but it is invaluable in the breeding season and the young will thrive on it. So this will pay golden dividends in April, May, June and July.

Essential Needs

In January handle each bird and blow the feathers on the chest apart and examine their bodies for any sign of ill health. All toenails are cut, and the feathers growing near to the vent are trimmed back but care is taken not to cut any of the vent guide feathers.

How to hold a canary

There is an art in catching and holding the bird when any examination is required; there should be no hurry or fluster but movement of the hand should be positive. Do not grip too tightly; it is better to let the bird go and to have another try.

To **examine either the back or the breast**, lay the bird on the palm of the hand; with the thumb across the neck it cannot escape and if the thumb and forefinger are touching, but allowing just sufficient space for the bird's neck, so that it cannot slip through, the body can be given perfect freedom, the palm of the hand bearing its weight.

Ensure that all the hens have a plentiful supply of cuttlefish bone. I stopped using grit fifteen years ago and fed charcoal instead. Since then I have not had a single thin-shelled egg or a hen that has become egg-bound.

Recording Results

I have recorded the results of the last three breeding seasons and it shows that from every clutch of eggs laid, I ended up with three young birds actually on the sticks. I believe the most important factor is the fitness of the birds at the time they are paired up.

After I have selected my breeding pairs, during the latter part of January, the pairs are held together in breeding cages and left together for at least a fortnight. Each hen gets to know the cock bird and normally no difficulties are experienced when the time comes to pair them up to breed.

NESTING PREPARATION

I use the earthenware type of nest-pan with a rounded lining sewed inside. The nest-pan rests on a ring made from *Twilweld* wire so that it is about 1 inch (2.5 cm) from the floor. There are several reasons for this:

1. Nest-pan is easy to lift in and out if this becomes necessary.
2. It is in a position where it is readily accessible to handle the eggs when the hen lays.
3. If a young bird is actually dragged out of the nest by the hen it cannot fall far and then only on the wood shavings.
4. When the young are 16–17 days old, if they stand on the edge of the nest and hop on to the floor of the cage, they can quite easily get back to the nest themselves.

For nest-building material old carpet underfelt of the non-fibrous type is recommended, which does not get under the small scales of the birds' legs and feet, causing them an injury. It should be washed before use.

FOOD HINTS

Canaries like carrots which can be pressed into the wires of the cage. It is an excellent food for your birds.

Another beneficial food is charcoal which is scattered on the floor of the cage for the hens. They spend much time eating and pecking at it. Hens also like soaked seed; not only does this help to vary the diet but it gets them used to the taste of it. This is essential because it is offered when they are feeding young.

With canary seed constantly rising in price it is much too expensive to waste so I have ceased to use canary mixture in the seed hoppers. Instead I put *plain* canary seed in the hoppers and *condition* seed and *wild* seed on the floor of the cage. It is surprising how much time the birds spend picking it over instead of sitting on the perch looking bored.

COMPARING RESULTS

A couple of years ago, in conversation with a friend, he asked me how many youngsters I had bred. I replied 'sixty' and he told me that he had reared fifty-six. However, when we compared notes we found that he had used twenty-four hens, some of which had laid three rounds of eggs.

I had used only eleven hens in the first round and six hens in the second round because part way through the second round I had been ill and my wife had not the time to spend in caring for the birds. There was therefore a big difference from a productivity point of view between my friend's fifty-six and my sixty!

KEEP YOUR BORDER ROOM TIDY

Canaries are, of course, kept and bred by non-exhibitors as well as keen fanciers who show their birds. During the past forty-six years I have visited many kinds of birdrooms. One I remember in particular was an old air-raid shelter in the backyard of a terraced house. It had been converted into a very nice little birdroom which contained half-a-dozen pairs of birds.

I have also seen canaries kept in a cellar adapted as a birdroom, in some very nice wooden structures in fanciers' gardens, as well as in brick-built rooms complete with double-glazing and the floors covered with smart-looking tiles.

5.2   *Double breeding cage built by Bill Chiltern.*

I have noticed that these birdrooms all have one common feature: namely the cage fronts incorporate holes for the seed hopper and drinker, which are both hung on the outside of the cage. I have found with these fronts there are two common weaknesses which are as follows:—

1. **Every time a bird puts its head into the drinker and enjoys a 'splash bath', water is scattered on to the birdroom floor. As most birdroom floors are covered with linoleum, the constant splashing of water on to one spot soon produces a stain or ugly mark on the linoleum.**
2. **If you cover the floor of your stock cage with either wood shavings or rough sawdust, the constant movement of the birds scatters the floor covering into both the drinker and seed hopper and also makes the birdroom floor untidy.**

A New Approach

One weekend some years ago, while out making my usual Sunday morning 'birdie' visits, I called to see two of my local society members who are both well known in the Canary Fancy. First, I went to see Bill Chiltern, who these days breeds and exhibits a good type of Norwich and who previously kept Glosters. In fact, he had the honour of staging the Best White Canary in Show at the National Exhibition in 1966 when it was held at Olympia. The bird he exhibited was an unflighted Consort hen. My second visit was to Gordon Adamson, who many will know is a well-known Gloster breeder, and who has twice judged Glosters at the Alexandra Palace.

As soon as I entered these fanciers' birdrooms, several things immediately caught my attention. For example, all the drinkers and seed hoppers and the floor were completely free from wood shavings, although the cage bottoms were covered with them, and the cleanliness was not due to a quick sweep round the floor before my visit.

So what was the secret of this tidiness? I remarked upon it to Bill Chiltern and he replied that both he and Gordon Adamson had discussed the problem of untidy birdrooms some years before. They had also looked into the problem of a bird's feet and tail getting soiled after it had been hand washed for a show. The result was that they completely redesigned their stock cage fronts.

Bill Chiltern, who is able to make a craftsmanlike job of whatever he puts his hand to, made a new type of wire cage front, with both the seed hopper and drinker holes positioned approximately 1 inch (2.54 cm) above the height of the perch.

The wire front was supported by a length of wood approximately $1\frac{1}{4}$ inches (3.17 cm) in depth and below this was a narrow gap sufficient to allow a hardboard tray to cover the whole of the bottom of the cage. The tray was designed to extend 2 inches (5 cm) from the front of the cage, and, as a result, collected any debris before it reached the floor of the birdroom or fell into drinkers on the cages below. Fixed to this piece of hardboard was a $\frac{1}{4}$-inch (approx. 6mm) piece of wood running the full width of the cage.

This particular design ensures that any bird wanting to feed or drink has to stand on one of its perches. The grit containers are half-round plastic utensils, fixed below and between the perches, at the back of the cages.

The softwood perches used inside the cages are $\frac{1}{2}$ inch (1.27 cm) × $\frac{3}{8}$ inch (9.25 mm). The head holes in the wire fronts are $1\frac{1}{8}$ inches (2.86 cm) in diameter. The actual cages are made from $\frac{1}{4}$-inch (9 mm) plywood but the backs are of 4-mm plywood. Hardboard is not used for this purpose for the simple reason that it does not allow the use of nails.

When making the cages, care is taken to ensure that all joints are glued as well as fixed with panel pins. This is to avoid any possible hiding places for mites.

The wire fronts are easily fixed into position, simply by cutting off the top pins and fitting on the inside of the cage an aluminium bracket with a turn button fixed at the top and bottom of the front. A wooden clothes peg is screwed, and also glued, to the side of the cage to hold a piece of cuttlefish bone.

A lot of thought has also been given to the use of the cages during the breeding season. The nesting boxes are $3\frac{1}{4}$ inches (8.25 cm) square (inside measurements); the bottom is covered with perforated zinc. A triangular shaped wired frame is screwed to the back of the wooden box to enable the receptacle to be positioned approximately $\frac{1}{2}$ inch (1.27 cm) away from the back of the cage.

The idea behind this is to ensure that when the young birds are old enough to void over the sides of the box, the back of the cage is not soiled by the droppings. The nest-box is hung into position by a U-shaped bracket secured to the back of the cage.

To keep the birdroom tidy, the first task each day only requires the use of a dustpan and handbrush to sweep away any bits that have fallen off the 2-inch (5 cm) painted hardboard strip which protrudes beyond the front of the cage. In fact, the birdroom floor does not require sweeping daily — only once or twice a week.

The wire fronts have been carefully painted and look quite impressive in appearance. The accompanying photograph shows the cage described (part of a double-breeder) complete with the nest-box.

AVOIDING CLAW DAMAGE

A wooden clothes peg may be used as a cuttlefish bone holder, but, like the greater majority of fanciers, I use a metal holder which is inserted between the wire fronts. However, I have known this type of holder to be responsible for more than one bird getting caught by its toe nails. There is another way of securing a piece of cuttlefish inside a cage, by the use of an S-shaped piece of wire. One end of the loop is pressed through the hard back of the cuttlefish bone and the other end is hung on the front of the cage. The wire ends do not protrude into the cage.

Last breeding season, when visiting fellow Canary fanciers' birdrooms, I was surprised to see that a number of them were not using feeding boards, either with or without countersunk pots. In one particular birdroom I noticed a single-breeder that contained three very promising young Borders, about four weeks old. They had recently been weaned from the parent birds. On careful observation, however, I saw that two of the youngsters had a stiff rear claw. I drew my friend's attention to this and was told that less than an hour before, both birds' feet appeared to be perfect.

We discussed this problem at some length and came to the conclusion that young birds must have damaged their feet while standing on a plastic food dish placed on the floor of the cage.

When I left my friend, he was about to start making feeding boards for his cages. For those thinking of making a feeding board complete with sunken container, I suggest they use glass salmon-paste containers or similar pots.

6.1 *Fawn and white hen with typical drinker attached to cage.*

6.2 *Wing of a bird partially stripped to show the insertion of the quills: feather patterns are all-important in breeding.*

CHAPTER 6

Preparing for the Breeding Season

CORRECT PAIRING

For fanciers who have had only a *limited experience* of canary breeding, it must be stressed that when breeding Borders you **pair a yellow bird to a buff one.** For more experienced fanciers I will explain later when to pair buff to buff and yellow to yellow.

With all breeds of canaries the first thing to remember when selecting your breeding stock is that the birds must show the correct **type.** Borders must have a fine silk-like feather quality, and to try and balance the quality of feather, we always pair yellow to buff.

Now, irrespective of whether you pair yellow to yellow or buff to buff, you will not improve the basic colour. Both the yellow and the buff feather colouring is controlled by a single gene, and transmitted in a separate hereditary unit. This is covered in Chapter 10.

I would recommend only one generation of either double yellow or double buff pairing. If you are breeding Greens or Cinnamons and your stock has very light, pencil-thin markings on their thighs, then try double buffing for one generation, this should result in young Greens or Cinnamons with thicker, darker thigh markings.

If, on the other hand, your Greens have thick black thigh markings which tend to reduce the amount of natural green background feather, then try double yellowing for one generation. This should produce birds which have a thinner and lighter pencilling on their thighs, and a more prominent green or cinnamon background feather.

Try this pairing for only one generation, unless you already have years of breeding experience behind you. If you try double buffing or yellowing for a consecutive number of breeding seasons, you will find that the all-important feather pattern will change and with it will go that most essential Border quality.

When selecting breeding pairs be quite sure that the two birds do not share the fault or weakness. Each breeding season, endeavour to

61

retain all the good points in your stock, and to improve one weak point in each pair each year.

How many fanciers realise how much the final breeding result depends upon the hen, for she will influence many factors, for example:

(a) She builds most of the nest.
(b) She produces a clutch of eggs and broods them for fourteen days with little exercise or time to feed.
(c) She feeds and rears the young ones for twenty-one days.
(d) She spends ten days constantly cleaning the nest.

A Six Point Plan

With this vast amount of work to be done I endeavour to build up the stamina and breeding conditions of the hens, with the following six-point plan:

1. Use only a good quality canary seed and red rape at the ratio of four to one.
2. Commencing twice a week, feed a half teaspoonful of good quality softfood, increasing it to five times a week at the end of January.
3. Provide a bath approximately three mornings every week.
4. Every other day feed either a little apple, carrot or unfrosted sprout and a little niger seed.
5. Provide plenty of good-sized pieces of cuttlefish bone. (I do not use grit as previously reported).
6. Put four drops of Parrish's Chemical Food in the water once a week.

No condition seed is fed until the beginning of March when the softfood is reduced by half and replaced by condition seed. Before pairing up, the hen should be kept in the cage where she should breed. This will make her feel in familiar premises and will naturally relax her.

When my hens begin to come into breeding condition, I set the thermostat at approximately 50°F (10°C). This is solely to ensure that any sudden cold spell does not give a frosty atmosphere in the birdroom at a time when the hen might be going to lay. To me, warmth means natural relaxation.

A useful Check List

Other useful points which can be associated with the egg are:—

1. Are you right handed or left handed? It is always advisable to place the

nest-pan or nest-box at the end of the cage where you can put in your hand and remove an egg easily without the possibility of breaking it.

2.   When the hen is in breeding condition it is especially important that she has a good supply of cuttlefish bone because just prior to laying you will find that she will peck out large quantities of it.

3.   Have you ever tried grating the cuttlefish bone or peeling it with a knife as you would an apple? Then it can be given to the hen in a softfood dish and you will find that she will eat quite a lot of it.

4.   The liberal use of cuttlefish bone will greatly help to reduce the possibility of soft-shelled eggs and, I feel, dead-in-shell also.

5.   Those breeders who are not able to give their feeding hens a fresh supply of softfood in the middle of the day during hot weather, should not use hardboiled egg. It is surprising how quickly it can 'go off'.

GOOD FEEDERS ARE VITAL

We breed Borders which we hope will have good heads on them but I maintain that it is even more important to produce young birds which will be good feeders when they themselves commence to breed the following season.

As an example, I will explain how my own birds fared last year. In the first round I decided to use only eleven hens and as a result there were thirty-four youngsters on the sticks.

It is a great advantage to have someone about who takes an interest in the birds and is able to give the feeding hens a fresh supply of food at midday. I am fortunate that my wife is quite an expert and can look after the birds when necessary.

When I was incapacitated for ten days forty-five young birds had to be looked after. In my absence, my wife coped and ended up with forty-two of them in good health losing only three birds.

I decided that breeding canaries under these conditions just was 'not on' so all the adult hens who had not, or had only partly, fed their young were disposed of, also all their young. I was then left with only seven hens. Next year was a very busy one at the office and I had little time to spend with the birds. However, six of the hens reared all their young with only routine attention from my wife. The rule to remember is:

Never, ever, try to breed from hens whose chicks had to be hand-fed. Only use those readily reared by the natural parent.

As each breeding season comes along we hear all too regularly of canary breeders losing many young birds between four and fourteen days old. I am convinced that the greater percentage of these losses could have been avoided. During the last three years it has been my good fortune to rear nineteen chicks out of every twenty hatched.

The essential requirement is to use those birds which are physically fit and have not had any illness during the winter months. Do not use birds that have been bred from poor feeders or whose parents produced more than one clear egg per nest. These two characteristics have to be bred for, just as much as; for example, a good head. I endeavour to get the cocks in breeding condition before the hens. During mid-December I commence to feed them a teaspoonful of good quality condition seed twice a week, increasing this to five times a week at the end of January. I also feed a little sprout leaves twice a week and soaked seed once a week.

NESTING MATERIAL

Equal care should be taken with all nesting material. The nest linings should be sterilised by placing them in a saucepan and putting them in a hot oven for five minutes. This is best done by arrangement with the lady of the house!

The nest pans or boxes should have been soaked in creosote for a day and then left to dry for a couple of months. It is a good idea to paste the linings in the nest pans, thus eliminating possible hiding places for red mite. For nesting material I use medicated wadding or some old non-fibrous carpet underfelt.

When both the cock and the hen are ready I pair them together in the morning, after having slightly moved the partition so that they could see a little of each other the previous day.

CAREFUL FEEDING

Many fanciers make a grave mistake by feeding their hens too richly at this time; the amount of egg-food should be reduced. Fanciers are sometimes under the impression that, because the cocks are in song, they do not require feeding well and the consequence can be infertile eggs.

In fact, during the month before they commence to breed, the cocks need feeding well to bring them into breeding condition. A safe rule is to provide each bird with a half-teaspoonful of softfood twice a week and the same amount of condition seed. The cocks will then be ready to pair about the same time as the hens.

It is a good idea to put a pinch of maw seed into the egg-food, especially for the cocks; a pinch of niger seed for the hens will also be beneficial.

PAIRING THE BIRDS

Resist desire to pair up your canaries too early

The time of the year at which birds should be put together varies according to circumstances. There is nothing in the whole round of canary breeding that requires such a cool head and the capacity for resisting temptation as the itching desire everyone has in the early spring to pair up their birds. It is only experience which makes the breeder wise in this respect. Nature, if we would but study her, has regulated all things well for the protection of both old and young birds and the breeder may go against her with disastrous results.

Egg-binding is far less likely to occur during warm weather and nothing is gained by being too anxious to pair the birds up early in the year, during the cold period. Even supposing one succeeds in getting the hens to lay and the eggs prove fertile and hatch out, there are odds against rearing the young.

Chicks are bountifully covered with a fine silky down-like feather which is quite sufficient for the first few days while the mother keeps them closely covered. She leaves the nest only for a few seconds for a little eggfood with which to feed the young. However, the chicks' down becomes thinner and, just before the feathers appear, the young birds are almost bare.

At this time the hen comes off the nest more frequently and remains off for longer periods and it is then the danger occurs, if the weather is really cold, as the featherless young get chilled. This can be avoided, to a great extent, if artificial heat is applied

Scores of infertile eggs are another result of pairing the birds too early. The symptoms of this desire to pair the birds generally show themselves on a sunny day after a period in the birdroom.

Perhaps we have picked a sprig or two of chickweed or young dandelion leaves and given our birds a taste of them and next day find some of the hens carrying the bare stalks and roots about the cage. It seems to have infused fresh life into the birdroom and also into the fancier. The weather continues mild and a walk is taken to gather fresh moss, etc, and unless the fancier knows the folly of giving way to this unexpected early sign of fine weather, he gets as restless as the birds.

We should remember that one swallow never made a summer and several fine days do not make a spring. The return of inclement weather makes us feel glad that we proceeded no further than a general clean up of cages and an examination of nesting material and

6.3 *Canary nest pans of various types: 1) Wire basket with plaited grass lining (Spain); 2) Pressed aluminium (Australia); 3) Moulded plastic (Spain); 4) Wooden pan for Norwich canaries (Australia); 5) Pan improvised from wire sieve (Malaysia); 6) Wooden box with gauze base (Britain); 7) Earthenware pan (Britain); 8) Cast iron pan with glued-in lining, dating from last century (Australia); 9) Pressed aluminium with gauze base.*

equipment. The old saying 'more haste, less speed', should be written over every birdroom door. I have known breeders lose half their hens by disregarding this.

Death from inflammation of the egg-passage, resulting in egg-binding, is the penalty for bringing birds into breeding condition before the dreary days of winter are past. One rule is never to pair up birds until they can see to feed at 6 a.m.

From 7 p.m. to 6 a.m. is a long fast, even supposing the young ones have full crops at 7 p.m. The policy of waiting until the spring is fairly advanced will therefore be obvious. **A safe rule, one based on common sense and long experience, is to wait at least until the middle of March, even if the weather is good and you live in a southern or south-western district, or until the beginning of April in the Midlands and northern districts.**

When a number of birds have been living together through the winter, the hens together in one large cage, they should be looked over early in the spring. Those intended for breeding purposes should be put apart and kept quiet in the cage in which they will breed.

The cocks will gradually be growing 'fresh', and will require to be caged in separate compartments. When they have been kept together in flights for lengthy periods, it is surprising how they remain amicable until one or more begin to come into high condition and full song. If there is any trouble, the birds causing it should be removed.

Assuming that things have gone on in an orderly fashion and that no jealousy has sprung up, the breeder should find himself into March with a nice stock of healthy birds. At this stage it is advisable to switch on the thermostatically controlled heating if a start is to be made during March or very early April.

At the best, March is a blustering month and April is not to be relied upon; east winds continue to harass us and winter does not depart without a struggle. In quarters thus made comfortable with the use of heating, the birds will soon show a desire to pair up.

Normally, it is the latter part of April before I commence to pair up the birds. Last December, however, I decided to start using a little heat in the birdroom, primarily for my own benefit. The result was that although the thermostat is only set at 42°F. (5.55°C), by the middle of January all my cocks, both young and old, were singing well.

On January 1st, I turned on the time-switch controlling the lighting so that the room was lit from 6 a.m. until 9 a.m. This meant that the birds enjoyed an extra three hours or so of daylight for feeding and exercise, and because of their forward appearance and feather the breeding season commenced a month earlier than usual.

READY TO BREED

When the birds are seen to be ready to breed, a nest-pan or nest-box should be put in the breeding cage adjacent to and level with one of the perches. Place the nest-pan between the two perches, with its bottom on a level with them or nearly so, so that the top of the nest is about 1 inch (2.5 cm) above the perches and there is about 1 inch between the actual nest and the perches.

This will allow the birds good standing room when feeding but this is not very important as the birds can and will stand on the nest-pan edge as often as the perch. Indeed, some breeders, including myself, never place their perches on the cross bar, but support one on the upper cross wire and the other on the middle cross bar, between the door frame and the side so the birds fly up to the nest.

As the birds get older, the nests are transferred to a low level, approximately 1 inch (2.5 cm) from the floor in case any fall out of the nest; they will then be able to get back on their own.

The situation of the perches, etc, is entirely a matter of preference, but there is an advantage in keeping the top of the nest above the perch if a perch is put near the nest. It enables the hen to leave her nest more readily and with less likelihood of dragging out her young, because the hen usually rises and steps on to the edge of the nest, and then hops up on to the perch.

During the last breeding season I used only carpet underfelt as nesting material. This, of course, was washed and dried thoroughly before use and I think it is quite true to say that my birds made some of the nicest nests that they have ever had and the cost was only minimal. Ensure that the underfelt does not include any fibrous material, but consists only of the soft woolly build-up. If you know of anyone who is having their carpet changed and has some old under-felt, be sure to try to get some.

Having cleaned out your cages thoroughly and gone over all your nesting equipment, it is time to think about putting the birds into the breeding cages. You must decide whether to breed from a pair of birds or whether the hen is to do all the rearing on her own and the cock is only there to fertilise the eggs.

When you first pair your birds together it is very necessary to spend an hour or so in the birdroom sitting still and making quite sure that the birds are getting along amicably. Occasionally one might turn on the other one in a vicious manner.

Last season I tried something new with three or four pairs, and that

68

was to give the hen the nest-pan complete with nest lining and let her get used to it for two or three days. It was interesting to see the birds get inside, spread out the wings and scuffle their feet at the bottom of the nest as though building. When I saw them doing this I gave them a little nesting material because until a hen begins to build in earnest she will waste the material to a very large extent.

If there is any moss or felting in the rack hung on the front of the cage protruding through the wires, a hen will continue to pull at it but if she is not really in condition she will throw it out of the nest and scatter it about the cage bottom.

This is all part and parcel of knowing when your birds are in breeding condition and actually ready to pair. The ideal is to pair your birds up and, after they have been together for twenty-four hours, give them a nest. A couple of days later provide the nesting material and within a week they should have built a lovely nest.

Within another week the hen should have laid a clutch of eggs. If, at the end of ten days the hen has neither laid nor has the appearance of going to nest, I would suggest that the pair be parted.

A small point worth mentioning is that before entering the birdroom it is advisable to tap on the door. Some people might enter a birdroom in a clumsy or noisy manner, perhaps causing a hen to claw holes in her eggs when she is frightened off her nest.

The removal of the eggs as laid and their substitution with dummy eggs, is something which I was told to practise over forty years ago and I have done so ever since. This is possibly what most canary breeders do but, as I have said before, in this hobby of ours there are no hard and fast rules. I know several people, one gentleman in particular, who never removes an egg as it is laid and yet he always seems to have a good breeding season.

The only argument I have heard in favour of allowing the hens' own eggs to remain is that those of wild birds are untouched until the full clutch has been laid. However, the bird in the wild does not become broody until she has laid a full clutch and, consequently, does not even remain near her nest, let alone brood the eggs. The difference is that a canary confined to a breeding cage can scarcely be said to be in a natural state like the bird in the wild. Never being allowed to lose sight of her nest and eggs she has every inducement to sit.

CONTINUE THE DIET

The diet as fed to the hen is continued, also the baths. On the second day introduce the nest pan and provide a little nesting material. As the eggs are laid, take them away each morning and on the evening of the day that the third egg is laid, the hen is sat.

Some fanciers may wish to use a cock with three or four hens, as I have done this year. I placed them together in a treble-breeder and left them for a few weeks prior to the breeding season so they were not complete strangers to each other when paired up.

When using one cock with three or four hens the same day, run him with one hen and let him stay until they have mated. If this does not look as if it will take place in the first two or three minutes, take him out of the hen's cage and put him back in his own cage for five or ten minutes, then try him with the next hen.

This year, using one cock and four hens, I had 21 eggs and I am delighted to say that the hens raised 21 young. While the hen was sitting I gave her a little softfood twice a week and a half teaspoonful of hemp on other days. This helped to maintain her strength and body temperature.

After hatching

When the chicks hatch out, the hen is given a little softfood twice a day for the first two days. At this stage the chicks have no digestive system of their own and the hen feeds them with a thick liquid known as crop juice.

As the chicks grow so does their stomach, digestive system and, of course, appetite. The amount of food given to the hen is therefore gradually increased for the first nine days. First give softfood, then a little watercress, bread and milk and, finally, softfood again. Each night before going to bed put a small dish of bread and milk in the cage ready for the hen first thing next morning.

It is always worth remembering that a little food given often is worth a lot more than two big feeds a day. The moral is to encourage your wife to take a little interest, particularly during the rearing season.

To help the hen to reduce the amount of nest cleaning while the chicks are only six or seven days old, it is advisable to build up the bottom of all the deep nests to make it easier for the young ones to void over the edge of the nest pan.

When the chicks are nine days old offer some soaked teazle and a little chickweed; if this is not available continue with watercress. This gives the hen added interest in feeding. A little Epsom salt is put in the drinking water for a few days at that period.

About this time, also place the nest pan near the floor of the cage with plenty of wood shavings or sawdust around it. If a chick is either dragged out of the nest accidentally by the hen or it falls out, it will not get hurt. If necessary it can be revived by placing it in the palm of your hand and gently breathing on it for a few minutes. Nine out of ten birds will be saved this way unless, of course, they have been left lying on the floor too long before you find them.

By the time that the chicks are seventeen days old the hen often wants to go to nest again. I then tie a short piece of string to the cage front and it is surprising how this keeps them occupied and prevents them plucking the young.

On the evening of the twenty-first day take the young ones away, putting on each one a split ring for identification. Nowadays I keep to a single colour and have the rings numbered.

The babies are placed in a single cage, the bottom of which is covered with newspaper. No perch is fitted for the first couple of days. A small dish of sloppy bread and milk, chopped up egg and a little chickweed is placed just inside the door. The paper is changed every day. A thin perch is introduced low down when they have been on their own for two or three days.

The diet for the first week or ten days consists of bread and milk, softfood and a little watercress. Soaked teazle or soaked seed is introduced at about five weeks, and a seed hopper containing red rape is put on the cage front when the birds are six weeks old.

Both softfood and watercress are fed until the moult is well under way or, in the case of watercress, until it is finished.

A show cage with one thin perch is hung on the front of the cage at five weeks and the young birds are quietly and gently handled. If for some reason you put your hand inside the cage, do it slowly, at the same time talking to the birds as if you were talking to your neighbour.

After the young ones are taken away the hen is left on her own for a few days, during which she bathes frequently. Softfood is not given, but a teaspoonful of condition food is provided each day.

Chickweed substitute

Because last summer was so long and hot, the chickweed died off before the second round youngsters hatched out; therefore, the natural food for the hens came to an abrupt halt. To offset this, a friend suggested to me that I put some small plastic bowls of well-rinsed and well soaked seed in the hot water cylinder cupboard, first undoing two sections of the lagging jacket at the top to let out a little heat into the cupboard. After being in this warm cupboard for three or four days at the most, the various seeds in the plastic containers had all commenced to sprout. Once hens developed a liking for this sprouting seed, rearing the young birds was no problem at all and the hens did not miss the chickweed.

71

7.1   *Hospital Cage.*

7.2   *Plastic bird bath — a daily bath should be given, especially during the breeding season.*

CHAPTER 7

Disappointments During The Breeding Season

Now a few words about breeding season disappointments. It may be safely said that there is not a breeder of canaries who does not have some disappointment or other during the breeding season. It may be a hen failing to lay, or laying soft-shelled eggs, or, in some cases, of long intervals between each egg. Some hens refuse to incubate their eggs, but the most disappointing of all is a hen that leaves a nest of eggs a day or two before they are due to hatch. Hens can become ill and die, or become egg-bound, often in the second round. The failure of some hens to feed their young is yet another problem, so it is always a good idea to mate up at the same time three or four different pairs of birds.

The breeder may ask what he should do when these troubles occur during the breeding season. You may well have paid special attention to your hens from the time they completed their moult until the start of the breeding season. It is at this point that the birds put on condition; in other words, put on fat, more particularly about the abdomen. This serves three purposes:

1. It provides a reserve of material on which the birds can draw
2. In cold weather it helps to protect the ovaries
3. It provides fat for the egg yolk when the ovaries become active

This layer of fat has a direct connection with the ovaries, on which much of the success of the breeding season naturally depends. If a healthy hen is examined during the winter, you will find this layer of yellow fat under the skin.

BREEDING PROBLEMS

Too Fat
There is little doubt that many of the problems experienced during the early part of the breeding season are due to fanciers pairing up their hens when they are *too* fat. I strongly advise fanciers never to

breed from a hen which is very fat.

If you examine a hen that is in condition, you will notice that almost the whole of the fat has disappeared and that the abdomen is like the rest of the bird's body. The hen is fit and ready to breed from.

Egg-eating

One of the difficulties that may occur during the breeding season is a hen that eats its own eggs. In these cases, it is wisest to get rid of the bird as it will never be an asset to you. Sometimes the cock bird is responsible for this, in which case it should be removed from the cage, leaving the hen to incubate the eggs and rear the young alone.

Refusal to Incubate

There are also hens that lay only one egg, then take no more notice of the nest. They hop from perch to perch, calling to the cock for food, or just mope about the cage. You should dispose of these hens too.

Another problem is the hen that lays a clutch of eggs and refuses to sit and brood them, while others hens sit for only part of the fourteen days incubation period. Sometimes this is due to lack of true breeding condition. I normally give the hens a second chance, as a sudden change in the weather can cause this particular trouble.

It is best to separate the birds for a week or ten days. Give the hen plain canary seed and a little bread soaked in milk and glucose, with a pinch of maw seed scattered on the top. Also, add a little extra salt to the drinking water. In most cases this should resolve the problem. When the hen shows signs of wanting to go to nest again, you should reintroduce the cock in the normal way.

Egg-binding

The arrival of the first egg is eagerly awaited by canary breeders. However, it can also bring the initial problem. For example, you may have noticed that one of the hens has finished its nest and you were expecting it to lay that morning. Instead you find it off the nest and looking really out of sorts. The hen may have the appearance of a ball of feathers; it is lifeless, has dull eyes and is very heavy round the vent. Suspecting the worst you catch up the bird as gently as possible, being careful to hold it by the shoulders.

With the bird lying on its back in the palm of your hand, gently blow the feather round the vent when it will readily be seen that the hen is egg-bound. To assist the bird to pass the egg, place her in a hospital cage in a temperature between 85°F (29.4°C) and 90°F (32.2°C).

If you do not have a hospital cage use a box-type cage and place it in front of a fire, ensuring that the inside of the cage does not get the direct force of the heat. With the assistance and comfort derived from the warmth, the bird should be able to pass the egg in the normal way during the next two hours.

If she does not, apply a little warm olive oil to the vent with the aid of a small paint brush. Egg-binding does appear to happen more frequently to some fanciers' birds than others and I feel that often it could have been avoided.

Now, what is egg-binding and how can it be prevented? Whenever I have discussed this problem with those of my friends whose birds have experienced it, in each case they say that the hen has been given a generous supply of niger seed and therefore the trouble should not have arisen. In other words their theory has been to give the hens a fairly oily diet to keep the bird's system supple.

I feel that this is wrong. First and foremost it should be appreciated that hens do not require an unduly oily diet, because they do not function like an internal combustion engine. I would suggest that the primary causes of egg-binding are (a) the hens not being in full breeding condition; (b) excessive internal body fat; (c) hens with a highly nervous disposition.

Contributory Causes

Assuming these to be the main contributory causes, how does one avoid them? This is a matter of common sense and being consistent with the daily birdroom duties as follows:

1. During the mid-winter months see that the hens are kept in a cage of sufficient size so that they have adequate wing exercise. Do not use a diet with too high a percentage of starch (such as nearly all canary seed). Decrease the amount of plain canary seed and increase the amount of sweet red rape which contains helpful oils.

If a particular hen appears to put on an excessive amount of body fat, reduce the amount of plain canary seed that is given and increase the quantity of red rape to give a mixture of 50 per cent of each. Roller Canary fanciers feed a very large percentage of red rape to their birds, but how often do you see an excessively fat Roller?

2. Before pairing up the birds make quite sure that the hen is really in breeding condition. Some fanciers might feel that this is easily said, but not so easy to judge. Spend a quiet half-hour just sitting still and watching.

Take note of the hens which carry nesting material at the back of the beak and whether the colour of the feathers round the beak and on the shoulders is emphasised. Also, observe those which droop their wings and call to the cocks, for nine times out of ten, they are the ones in true breeding condition.

Give a daily bath of cold water. Birds love a bathe — or, at least, the majority do. Some fanciers do not introduce the cock until the hen has almost completed the nest on her own.

3.   Often a hen will become egg-bound on the second egg (of the first or second round) although the first egg appeared to be laid without any undue difficulty. To me there is only one explanation: when the yolk drops off the egg sac and commences to pass down the oviduct, collecting the white and the shell, the hen feels a certain amount of discomfort. As the egg is laid the discomfort increases, and the hen's nervous system becomes tense.

Those of us who have sat quietly in the birdroom about 5.30 a.m. and watched the hen which was expected to lay that morning, will have seen her half rise in the nest and partly extend her wings. She will remain like this for a minute or so before gradually relaxing again on the nest after the egg is laid.

In a hen of a highly-strung nature the discomfort of passing the egg has a pronounced effect, with the result that when the next egg is on the point of being laid the bird becomes tense, and its muscles tighten. The egg cannot then be laid.

It is only when the nervous system is soothed and the tension relaxed by placing the bird in a warm hospital cage that the egg is laid naturally. In my opinion, hens that are of a highly-strung and nervous nature should be excluded from the breeding programme.

The real anwer to the egg-binding problem is proper housing conditions and feeding, and only pairing up when the hen is in true breeding condition. Additionally, one should use only hens of a naturally relaxed nature which are also keen and sharp in their ways.

Barren hens

Barren hens are birds that fail to lay. Sometimes young hens fail to lay during their first breeding season, but in the second season raise some fine young birds.

The generally accepted rule is that if a hen does not lay at all during a breeding season, she will most probably be permanently barren. Old age is the most common reason for this, but it can also be the result of a bad moult.

It is surprising how barren hens will go to nest and make excellent foster mothers. They incubate the eggs and rear the young birds as if they were their own.

Infertile Eggs

When a hen has been sitting for six days, you can examine the eggs to see how many are fertile. Some breeders do this as a necessary precaution against a hen sitting the time out on clear eggs, resulting in the loss of a possible third round. This practice is not recommended as an over-worked hen will, as a rule, be that much less effective in the following breeding season. Also, it could easily adversely affect the bird during its all-important moult.

It is far better to let the hen sit through the full incubation period, even on a nest of infertile eggs. Allowing a hen to sit out the full, natural period will prevent the next clutch of eggs coming along too quickly. When a hen is not allowed to sit out the full incubation period the next clutch is often infertile, because the bird has been forced to lay again too soon.

Fertile Eggs

You can tell at a glance if an egg is fertile, without handling it excessively, because it will have an opaque appearance. If the egg is seen a day later in strong light, the network of blood vessels can be traced spreading over the inner surfaces of the shell. After another day, the fertile egg becomes entirely opaque.

If in a nest of four or five eggs there are one or two that are infertile, they should *not* be removed. When the young ones have hatched out, these eggs will help to support them in the nest. The eggs can remain until the young are sitting on the edge of the nest-pan.

There are several reasons for infertile eggs. If the hen is in perfect breeding condition, not too fat, and lays the eggs at correct intervals, it is to the cock bird that we must look for the cause.

Examine it carefully to see if it has reached breeding condition by gently blowing on the feathers of the abdomen just below the breast bone. If it is in breeding condition, the abdomen should be a little sunken and the vent should obtrude distinctly.

If the abdomen is bulging and yellow, place the bird in a flight cage and give it a little rape seed, canary seed and plenty of greenfood, preferably dandelion, supplying both leaves and split roots. When this fat condition is reduced, it should then fertilise the eggs.

If the cock appears to be in good breeding condition, check whether the feathers around the vent are too thick and long, thus preventing a successful mating. Trim as many of these feathers as you think necessary, being careful not to cut away the actual guide feathers.

This should be done for both sexes early in February, before putting them in their breeding cages. If you are uncertain which are the guide feathers, you should first seek the advice of an experienced canary breeder. Needless to say, great care should be taken not to cut the actual bird with your scissors.

Another cause of infertile eggs is insecure perches. Yet another is the hen that insists on sitting on the nest and calling the cock.

Failure to Hatch

There is nothing more disappointing than the failure of a hen to hatch out fertile eggs. This may be due to the following causes:

1. **Lack of moisture**
2. **Failure on the part of the hen to turn the eggs in the nest while they are being incubated**
3. **Lack of vigour in the parent**

Pre-use of the bath will prevent the first cause and the second can usually be avoided by placing a piece of cardboard on part of the cage front to shelter the sitting hen. The third case can be prevented only by making sure that your pair of birds are strong and healthy when they are brought together. One other cause of unhatched eggs is the hen not having the correct body temperature when sitting, which is due to lack of condition.

REARING PROBLEMS

Feather-plucking

When the young birds are about ten to twelve days old, the breeder must be on the watch for any signs of the hen plucking them. This

7.3   Numbered egg drawer

usually takes place during the latter part of the first round, and is one of the most annoying things that can occur during a breeding season. You will find that the odd hen will pluck one of its young in order to start building a second or third round. In these cases, either separate the young ones by using a wire slide, so that the hen can continue to feed them, or make use of an anti-peck spray.

Breeders will appreciate the necessity of taking a careful look at all new nests being built to see that they are not lined by feathers taken from the young birds. Should a hen start to pluck the young birds, it will continue to do so unless you take action quickly.

You will find that not only does it pluck out the feathers but also the new quills as they grow out of the skin. I have found that this can sometimes be stopped by tying a 6 inch (15 cm) long piece of soft string to the inside of the cage-front near a perch.

It is not just the hens that develop this mischievous habit; cocks are equally guilty of the practice. When these cases occur, the same precautions should be taken.

If you are certain that only the cock is doing the feather-plucking, remove it from the breeding cage, returning it only four or five times a day so that it can mate with the hen. After mating, it should be put back in its own cage. You will find that by doing this, the hen will successfully rear the young alone.

I have found that the habit of feather-plucking most frequently occurs when four, five or six young birds are housed in a double breeder to moult out. In these cases, it can take on a much more serious form, when the offender does not content itself with plucking just the small feathers, but also plucks the strong quill feathers from the wings and tail.

When these strong quills are growing they are full of liquid and, if pulled out, will bleed. This trouble generally occurs before the feathers are fully grown. The culprit should be removed at once. It is usually easy to detect the culprit as it will have traces of blood on its beak and face.

Diarrhoea

If young birds beginning to feed themselves are troubled with diarrhoea, stop their greenfood immediately. Be sure that all food is clean and sweet, the water pure and the drinking vessels clean. One drop of castor oil placed directly into the beak will clear up the bowels.

If the birds are on softfood, add to it at each meal sufficient arrowroot to cover a penny piece. A little warm water added to the drinking water is also beneficial, or the water can be substituted by strong cold tea for a few days.

If the young birds take on a puffed appearance, their diet should be restricted to plain canary seed, plus a small amount of bread soaked in milk mixed with glucose and made fresh each day. About 10 drops of tincture of rhubarb can be added to about a cup of drinking water until the birds regain their normal appearance.

A WORD OF WARNING

It is always important to enter your birdroom quietly and calmly, as a startled sitting hen can easily put its toe nails through an egg. If it becomes necessary to catch up a bird, a sharp, decisive pounce of the hand will usually be all that is required to capture a canary. Do not be in a hurry or a fluster.

To examine a bird's back or chest, lay the bird on the palm of the hand with your thumb across the neck. The correct way of holding a canary without ruffling its plumage is to take the tips of the wings and the root of the tail between the thumb and fingers. If held in this way there is no fear of it escaping.

BREEDING STRATEGY

It does not follow that the best birds from the exhibition point of view will be bred from parents which exhibit more virtues and fewer faults than another pair. But, in the long term, it is safe to say that greater success ensues by continuing to pair birds of a good exhibition standard to those that breed well but are of inferior appearance.

You may possess an excellent Yellow cock that has done well and is still capable of winning, but which has always been inclined to breed undersized young. You can, quite justifiably, retain some of the offspring for breeding with beneficial results; if properly paired, the desired size may possibly be recovered.

If, however, there is no increase in size in the third generation, or if size is further diminished, attempts to regain it should be discontinued. It is a waste of time to carry on in the hope that some day a return to normal size will occur.

CHAPTER 8

Tips for Novice Breeders

COMMON PROBLEMS

Drinkers
When training young birds in show cages they have to learn to use a drinker for the first time which is in a different position from those in the stock cages. Start by placing the show cage drinker in position and the one in the stock cage three-quarters of an inch below its normal level. When the youngsters have become used to drinking from it at this level, raise the perch a little each day until the space between the drinker and the perch is the same as it is in the show cage.

Damaged or cracked eggs
These can be 'repaired' by applying two or three coats of nail varnish. If the damage is soon spotted and the crack treated without delay, it is more than likely that the chick will emerge when it is due to hatch out. I have even known of one instance when a small piece of shell had been removed without damaging the membrane. The surface was treated with nail varnish and the young bird hatched out in the normal way.

Hen that will not return to her nest
To encourage her to go back to her chicks at nightfall, try removing all the perches from the cage and as a result she should return to her nest.

Perches
In my opinion softwood perches are by far the best for everyday use as they become rough when they are rubbed and scrubbed, whereas the surface of hardwood perches eventually become shiny. Those of softwood tend to have a little more give in them when a bird alights, which, of course, has an advantage. The best way to ensure that a canary gets a good grip on either kind of perch is to 'scar' the wood by running an old hacksaw blade along the face.

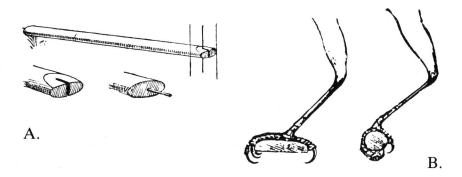

A.

B.

8.1 Perching arrangements: A. Attaching the perch.
B. Bird gripping correctly on suitably shaped dowel perching.

8.2 Typical canary nest pan with rim for bird to grip on to.

Selling

A little caution is necessary when a final decision is made on which birds should be sold. Take, for example, an unflighted hen which in a season laid two clutches of eggs from which six youngsters were raised and yet the following year she failed to bring off a single chick. In such a case, I would suggest that the bird is retained and she is tried again next breeding season. If, on the other hand, you are thinking of introducing new blood into your stock, you should bring in one or two cock birds.

'Going light'

A remedy Australian fanciers use is to add four or five drops of flat *Coca-Cola* to the drinking water. In Australia they are firm believers in this remedy and their birds seldom appear to 'go light'.

Slip claw

To those who are new to canary culture, the term may require a little explanation. Years ago it referred only to the rear claw which has lost its ability to grip. If not given immediate attention it would curl forward under the front toes. The best treatment is to hold the claw backwards so that it is flat against the leg, then, using either a piece of soft wool or Sellotape, fasten the claw in that position and leave it for a fortnight. When the bandage is removed, in nine out of ten cases it will be found that the claw will be able to grip a perch in the normal way.

There is also a somewhat similar condition that is commonly called **'stiff hind claw'**. This term is self-explanatory. At first it might not appear to be much of a problem; however, it can be most difficult to overcome. When any birds develop this trouble the first thing to do is to remove all the perches from the cage for a fortnight. At the end of this period the cage is fitted with a single wooden perch or a length of rope $1\frac{1}{4}$ inches (3 cm) in diameter. If rope is used, tie one end to the wire front and fasten the other to the back of the cage with a drawing pin, making sure the rope is taut.

In order to perch properly the bird has to maintain its balance and in so doing, endeavours to grip with its defective claw. It is when young birds develop this fault while still in the nest that the weakness of the joints and muscles quickly sets in. At that stage the breeder cannot see the youngsters' feet so when they start to stand on the rim of the nest-pan, he should make a point of checking that the feet are gripping properly.

LINE BREEDING

Recently, I have been asked by several fanciers who are in their second or third years with Borders to explain in simple terms just what **line breeding** is and how they have to go about putting it into practice. Many newcomers are, in fact, confused by the term.

By listening to lectures at local club meetings and reading various articles, they are convinced it is the best way of producing good stock. This, of course, is perfectly true but these enthusiasts with a few birds are apt to become confused and go back to random pairing because, to them, a line breeding system seems all too complicated.

Let us take one pair of birds, for example. If, in your opinion and that of an experienced fancier, the best of two particular Borders is the cock bird, then this one would be the 'line' bird. After breeding from the pair, select from the youngsters the best young hen, which, the following year, would be paired back to its father.

From this particular mating, once again select the best young hen. The third year the original 'line' bird will be mated to the latest young hen which, in fact, is a grandfather x grand-daughter mating. If, after breeding from the adult cock for three seasons, it is still very fit, the bird can be used again for the fourth year.

On the other hand, if you decide that it may be past its best performance, do not use it again in the line breeding programme. Instead, select from the latest batch of youngsters the best young bird. This youngster now becomes the 'line' bird for future matings.

The following season pair this bird to an unrelated bird; it may come from another pair in the birdroom, or alternatively, be purchased from another breeder. Select a good bird which will be used for one year. Pick one which is strong in the characteristics that are lacking in the 'line' bird. Avoid selecting a hen used previously in the line breeding programme because the idea of the mating is to introduce fresh blood to boost stamina and strengthen.

Continue as before but keep the best young hen and the following year pair it to your 'line' cock that has been retained. Keep only the best young hen for pairing to this cock bird. After the third year, select the best young bird as the 'line' bird.

It is seen that the three (or four) year cycle repeats itself, one line bird being used for three partners. By using two 'line' birds you will have at least six breeding seasons to help you establish some uniformity throughout your stock.

Unfortunately, from time to time accidents do happen, so if you have the space available ensure that your line breeding system does not come to a sudden end as a result of the death of a key bird.

8.3   Adult variegated yellow hen.

8.4   Unflighted variegated yellow hen.

Therefore, keep a brother of your 'line' cock in reserve, and each year when you select the best young hen retain a sister as a standby.

FEEDING

During the moulting period I have gone out in the countryside every other day and collected a fresh supply of green seeding docks, seeding grasses (the type that grow under trees and are small in size), shepherd's purse and that favourite of the birds, plantain or rat's tails. To those fanciers who live in a large town or city and who are at work during the day, I suggest that part of the weekend should be spent in the nearest countryside gathering as many of these weeds as you can. I think it is so much nicer if you take your wife and family with you and make it a family outing.

The reasons for collecting quantities of seeding dock, and other plants are twofold. Not only does it give the birds a liberal supply of different supplementary seeds and varied vitamins, but it also helps to enhance the natural colour of the birds and puts a lovely sheen on their feathers.

Last spring I called to see a farmer friend who had used up all his hay. I swept up what was left of the seeds and bits and pieces and put it in a large hessian bag. When the adult birds commenced to moult I put a handful of these hay loft sweeping on the bottom of the cages.

It kept the birds active and interested in picking over the seeds when normally they would have been sitting on the perches looking bored. It was also noticeable how much longer the seed in the hoppers lasted with considerable saving in the feed bill.

Recently, I went to see a friend who gave me a useful tip. He sows black rape during the first week in September, scattering it on the soil and gently raking it in. It is then well established and will even grow during the winter. In the spring, when the first round youngsters are in the nest, the growing rape will develop a yellow flower of which the feeding hens are very fond. They will readily feed it to their young, which seem to thrive on it.

When you have gathered and used up all the flowers you can start giving the feeding hens the young green leaves of the rape plants. Several of my friends grow black rape instead of using chickweed as this normally is either not available or dies off at the end of May if we get a sunny spell.

86

DEVELOP YOUR OWN QUALITY BIRD

While the main aims of our hobby are keeping, breeding and exhibiting Border Canaries, or whatever birds are kept, meeting fanciers and making friends is equally important. One encounters many kinds of fanciers, including, unfortunately, those few whose main interest would appear to be to make money out of their fellow fanciers.

Generally speaking, they have a bird which has had a good show season, usually one which has been bought from a breeder who did not appreciate its true show potential.

The fancier who has bought the bird, sometimes at a high price, may have bred only about thirty birds during the whole of the breeding season. He then buys forty or fifty birds from other fanciers and these he sells as his own stock to anyone enquiring about purchasing new stock on the strength of the performance of his winner.

We should take care not to let this minority type of fancier dampen our enthusiasm in any way, but instead we should, to use a ladies' phrase, 'shop around'. Then, after having thought about the birdrooms and birds you have seen, you can next select one particular fancier whose birds have appealed to you most.

You should be careful not to pay high prices. I suggest that the most you should consider is £10, with a £10 ceiling for an unflighted bird.

Five years ago my wife came to me at a show and said that she had bought a bird for me. It was a Fawn and White hen, small, narrow across the shoulders and head and with a very flat back.

From this particular Fawn and White I bred a Self Blue hen a little better in size than its mother. In four breeding seasons I bred a Blue and White hen from his family and a Cinnamon hen, both of which have taken major awards at open shows.

The moral of this story is not to spend a lot of money buying one particular bird; instead pay £5 or £6 for a less outstanding specimen and then spend three or four breeding seasons in developing a bird of quality. It really is most rewarding.

*9.1   How to handle a show cage while judging:
      A. Correct method.   B. Incorrect method.*

CHAPTER 9

Exhibiting Your Canaries

One of the pleasures of canary breeding, exhibiting, can be greatly increased by joining a Cage Bird Society; there is at least one in every town in the U.K. . You will often find that the smaller the town the more active is the society, which often has a very active social side. As your experience grows, then is the time to join a specialist society which caters for your variety of canary.

SELECTING BIRDS FOR SHOW

In selecting which of your birds are up to show standard, it is advisable to select several and place them in cages as at a show. With the cages standing side by side and your birds steady, select only the ones which, in your opinion, are nearest to the ideal Border, and then send those birds to the show. It is as well to do this at least a week before the show entry day closes. The birds which you have selected should be provided with a shallow amount of water in which to have a bath. This will assist the birds to preen every feather into its correct position.

BREEDING FOR EXHIBITION

Border canaries offer the breeder almost unlimited scope and interest once you make a start to being a regular exhibitor, be it **Novice** or **Champion** status. If, after two or three years of exhibiting, a Novice decides that from an exhibiting point he wishes to go right to the top, he must remember that this pinnacle can only be reached with Borders which he himself has bred. To do this he will have to have first-class breeding stock and he should follow the line breeding principle. But remember, do not allow sentiment to over-rule your better judgment when it comes to selecting breeding pairs. Use only those birds which are 100 per cent and do not have a common failing, whose mother always laid a clutch of four or five fertile eggs, and was also an excellent feeder; both parents must excel in type and feather.

89

Remember that it is equally important to breed for fertility and feeding as it is to breed the correct type. When purchasing any new stock only buy unflighted birds, unless it is from someone you know personally and respect. There are some Champion breeders who buy in stock and sell again as their own strain.

The United Kingdom is the only major country where it is not compulsory for all Borders to be close rung, with coded rings that can be obtained only through a specialist Border Society. In my view it is time we British Border breeders close rung all our young birds like the rest of the world; it would ensure that money does not buy winners.

HAND WASHING BORDERS

When you are exhibiting your Borders it is essential that not only are they properly trained to show themselves off with confidence, but you, the exhibitor, have to ensure that the Borders' plumage is immaculate, with no soiled and dirty feathers, especially around the neck. When a bird has soiled feathers you should hand wash it one week before the show.

To hand wash a bird you must first make the following preparations:

1. Obtain a good quality hair shampoo then, using a basin, mix some of the shampoo with warm water;

2. Next, get two bowls of warm water in which you will rinse the bird after washing;

3. You will require a third bowl of rinsing water to which you should add a little vinegar, mixing well together. The purpose of the vinegar is to neutralise any soap left in the feathers. If any soap is left in the feathers when they dry out, the feathers will be stuck together. Switch on your hospital cage and set the temperature at 85°F (30°C).

First catch up the bird and hold it in your left hand; you will find the back of the neck and its tail feathers are always the most soiled. You now use either a very old shaving brush or a small piece of sponge, dipped into the liquid shampoo, to soak the bird's neck. Then support the tail by your wrist and give that a soak also; the idea being to loosen all the dirt in the neck and tail feathers first.

Caution! When washing a bird brush the feathers only in the direction of head to tail, this is MOST important. Then, starting with the head, you commence to wash the bird, doing its back first. When you reach the wing feathers, support them, with your first finger and thumb, on your wrist. Then turn the bird over and wash that part. When you have completed the washing, hold the bird with only its head showing above your first finger and thumb. Then immerse the whole of the bird in the first rinsing water and with a clean wet sponge gently wash out all the soapy water. Next, repeat this with rinses two and three, after which, with a dry cloth, wipe off all the surplus water. Then fold a warm cotton cloth round the bird and put it in the hospital cage.

The whole of this should only take two minutes. After the bird has been in the heated hospital cage for five to ten minutes, remove the cotton wrapping. When the bird has been in the hospital cage for two hours it should by then be completely dry and its normal self. Then switch off the cage and let it cool down gradually during the night, and the next morning each bird should be returned to its own individual stock cage.

On the second, third and fourth days, give the bird a gentle, very misty spray with chilled water. This will encourage it to preen all its feathers into their correct positions. When judging a number of Borders from which you have to select a **Best Border in Show**, nothing looks nicer than an expertly hand washed bird.

A word of advice. If you personally have never hand washed a Border, then when you do, it should be one which in your opinion is surplus to requirements.

SHOW PROMOTING

Overall requirements

Bird shows are of such frequent occurrence that there is little need to enter into the details of their management, or their promotion. A well-lit, roomy hall, free from draughts, is most desirable for the well-being of the exhibits and any neglect in the selection of such a place frequently affects the entries at future shows. The hall selected should, if possible, be situated in a good thoroughfare so as to attract the attendance of the public and thus make the show a financial success.

A good example of the type of hall that should be in one's mind is that used by the **British Border Fancy Canary Club** at their annual show. This is the Civic Hall, Winsford, where, when the staging is set out and 2,200 birds are on display, you could drive a car comfortably between the rows of staging and still not touch the fanciers looking at the birds on show.

The secretary or show manager should have some experience of the work that he or she is undertaking or else be very well supported by experienced members. A complete set of show account books, so

A.   B.

C.   D.

9.2   *Four basic stages in handwashing a Border:*
    A. Correct way to hold bird   B. Dipping bird into water
    C. Lifting bird from water   D. Drying bird

9.3   Equipment for hand washing Borders.

9.4   Six compartment Dewar show cage carrying case.

that the details of everything connected with the exhibition are at the secretary's fingertips, are a great asset. Good temper and tact are also valuable assets in tiding over difficulties and getting the best out of the working staff.

At such events every member of the society, whether or not on the committee, ought to render all possible assistance and not, as is too often the case, allow the lion's share of the work to fall on about half a dozen willing workers.

Members of the committee do not always realise the responsibility incurred through their names, figuring on the official list. While we well know that too many cooks spoil the broth, this is only true if all want to be head cook, not if each is willing to take the place allotted to him under a chief steward.

STAGING

In recent years much improvement has been made in regard to staging, and this has been of the greatest assistance to the judges in carrying out their duties, as exhibits staged at a proper height are seen more easily and to greater advantage. It is all the better for the public and, perhaps of even greater importance, for the birds themselves.

Picture the nervous strain on birds, even if they are steady and used to the excitement of shows, when they are staged on tables as low as 2 feet 6 inches (76 cm) high with a throng of people peering over the top of them.

The best staging is that of the two or three tier principle. It saves space and gives the show a neat appearance. The bottom tier or shelf should be about 3 feet to 3 feet 6 inches (91 cm to 106 cm) from the floor and 7 inches or 8 inches (18 cm or 21 cm) wide for the cages to stand on. This will afford greater protection to the birds and cages than a narrower shelf.

The next shelf is arranged behind and about 10 inches to 12 inches (26 cm to 31 cm) above the first one and the third is a similar height above the second. The rest of the shelves are arranged on the lean-to principle.

Two shelves can be placed on opposite sides in like manner with the third as an apex at the top of both sides. This arrangement permits us to stage a large number of birds in a smaller space.

On the two lower tiers on either side such birds as Norwich, Lizards, British and other birds of position should be placed. Varieties such as Yorkshires and Borders which are exhibited in open wire cages, would be better staged on the two top-most tiers. If the

94

front of the staging is draped from the bottom tiers to the floor a neat finish is given to the exhibition.

Whatever form of staging is adopted, sufficient space must be allowed in the aisles between the exhibits so that several people can pass without inconvenience. The staging must be arranged so that as much light (daylight and artificial) as possible is thrown on the birds.

All the staging should be erected before the birds arrive and the space measured off for each class. This can easily be calculated by taking the number of entries in each class and allowing for the average sized show cage of that particular variety.

Numbering

As each class is measured off, its class number should be affixed to the staging; as the exhibits are unpacked they can at once be put in position. They should be unpacked in a perfectly draught-free area. As each cage is taken out its number should be called over to the official in charge, who should check it with the official entry list and direct where it is to be staged.

For this purpose the show manager or chief steward should be familiar with the arrangements of all the classes and in this way one checker can keep several unpackers at work without confusion and saving much time. It is most important to check the birds off as they arrive in order to discover which are absent. A note should be kept of all absent birds and this should be given to each judge.

As soon as each package or carrying case is emptied, the labels should be reversed or the top half removed so that the exhibitor's address is readily visible. The carrying case can be put in its appropriate place. If a fancier has sent food, be particularly careful to ensure that his birds have got a plentiful supply.

Providing Water

It is most important that every bird should have water before leaving the unpacking table and not be kept without it until after judging. The neglect of this makes judging most difficult because the birds are seeking a drink instead of showing themselves off before the judge.

In giving water, however, care should be taken to only half-fill the drinkers; if more water is allowed the chances are that the birds will begin to splash and drench themselves in it and quite possibly would not be dry when judged. Many a prize has been lost through not taking this precaution which is unfair to exhibitors. After the class has been judged the drinkers can be filled up.

CLOSE OF SHOW

Careful packing and quick despatch of birds at the close of the show, prompt payment of prize money and despatch of specials, all ensure greater support at a future show. A good schedule and specials list help to increase the entry.

SHOW PUBLICITY

To advertise a show may seem to some to be an unnecessary expense but this is not so. A few well worded inches in the Fancy press, such as *Cage and Aviary Birds*, three or four weeks before the show takes place, will not only increase the entry but also induce fanciers and others to attend the show.

Posters and hand-outs distributed locally by members do much to secure the attendance of the general public. The outlay and advertising, if done properly, will undoubtedly be well repaid.

We know from experience that the liability attached to a show makes its officials study expenditure carefully. This is as it should be but, nevertheless, cheapness should not be their first consideration. Qualified judges whose decisions meet with the general approval of exhibitors, even if costing a little more, are usually the cheapest in the end for they secure a good entry.

Again, while no judge will complain of a good day's work, he should not be overtaxed. Give him, if possible, a good start in the morning when he is fresh and the light is good, the show room quiet and the birds not excited. The duty of a judge, it should be emphasised, is to adhere to the recognised standard and not any pet notions of his own.

Good Reporters

People reporting shows for the Fancy Press have as important a duty as the judge if we are to have a reliable report. If not, then it is better to have no report at all rather than one which is misguiding to inexperienced exhibitors and readers unable to attend the show.

It has been suggested by some that judges as well as reporters should be supplied with a catalogue while officiating. I should be sorry to see such a practice in vogue for I maintain that if a judge cannot pick out the best exhibits without the aid of a catalogue he does not possess the necessary ability.

The same applies to the reporter. When taking his notes at a show he should use a schedule from which to get the headings of the classes, and other details then write out his critique. Afterwards he should

For the benefit of the novice fancier who may be considering showing, an extract is given below of the classes for the Border Canary at the National Championship Show held annually in Britain.

CHAMPION BORDER CLASSES
74 Yellow Cock, clear or ticked
75 Yellow Hen, clear or ticked
76 Buff Cock, clear or ticked
77 Buff Hen, clear or ticked
78 Yellow Cock, variegated
79 Yellow Hen, variegated
80 Buff Cock, variegated
81 Buff Hen, variegated
82 Yellow Cock, 3-parts dark
83 Yellow Hen, 3-parts dark
84 Buff Cock, 3-parts dark
85 Buff Hen, 3-parts dark
86 Yellow or Buff Cock, Cinnamon variegated
87 Yellow or Buff Hen, Cinnamon variegated
88 Cinnamon Yel. Cock, self or foul
89 Cinnamon Yel. Hen, self or foul
90 Cinnamon Buff Cock, self or foul
91 Cinnamon Buff Hen, self or foul
92 Green, Yellow Cock, self or foul
93 Green, Yellow Hen, self or foul
94 Green, Buff Cock, self or foul
95 Green, Buff Hen, self or foul
96 Unfli. Yel. Cock, clear or ticked
97 Unfli. Yel. Hen, clear or ticked
98 Unfli. Buff Cock, clear or ticked
99 Unfli. Buff Hen, clear or ticked
100 Unfli. Yellow Cock, clear or ticked
101 Unfli. Yellow Hen, green, variegated
102 Unfli. Buff Cock, green, variegated
103 Unfli. Buff Hen, green, variegated
104 White Cock, clear or ticked
105 White Hen, celar or ticked
106 Blue, Fawn, or var. White Cock
107 Blue, Fawn, or var. White Hen
108 Even-marked Cock or Hen (including Whites).

EXHIBITORS IN CLASS 108 MUST STATE COCK OR HEN ON ENTRY FORM

NOVICE BORDER CLASSES
109 Yellow Cock, clear or ticked
110 Yellow Hen, clear or ticked
111 Buff Cock, clear or ticked
112 Buff Hen, clear or ticked
113 Yellow Cock, variegated
114 Yellow Hen, variegated
115 Buff Cock, variegated
116 Buff Hen, variegated
117 Yellow or Buff Cock, 3-parts dark
118 Yellow or Buff Hen, 3-parts dark
119 Cinnamon, Yellow or Buff Cock, self or foul
120 Cinnamon, Yellow or Buff Hen, self or foul
121 Green, Yellow or Buff Cock, self or foul
122 Green, Yellow or Buff Hen, self or foul
123 Unfli. Yel. Cock, clear or ticked
124 Unfli. Yel. Hen, clear or ticked
125 Unfli. Buff Cock, clear or ticked
126 Unfli. Buff Hen, clear or ticked
127 Unfli. Yellow Cock, variegated
128 Unfli. Yellow Hen, variegated
129 Unfli. Buff Cock, variegated
130 Unfli. Buff Hen, variegated
131 White Cock, any variety
132 White Hen, any variety

9.5   *Extract from a show schedule.*

secure a catalogue for the names of the respective exhibitors.

Catalogues showing the prize winners should be on sale soon after judging is completed. Until these are ready there should be a supply without the award sheets in them. A certain number of stewards should always be in the show hall keeping a watchful eye on the exhibits and seeing that all is well.

If the show is of a longer duration than one day, at about 8.30 a.m. on the morning of the second day, all the birds should receive fresh water and seed.

MAJOR SHOWS ARE SUPERB BUT DO NOT NEGLECT THE 'LOCALS'

Apart from national, area and country shows, exhibitors have, what I regard as the backbone and lifeblood of the Fancy, the local cage bird societies' show. If all clubs promoting open shows were to bear this in mind, and not attempt to out-do each other or act bigger than their real support justifies, fewer would make a financial loss and their events would receive much better support from the fanciers in a 30 to 50 mile radius. Travel costs have increased so much that most fanciers can now afford to travel 100–200 miles and more only to major events, at which to see the cream of the variety which they keep and to meet old friends, of course.

Sending our birds to compete at open shows is what the hobby is all about, provided we select shows within a reasonable distance of our own homes and make a point of visiting such shows.

If the Fancy as a whole takes this line of approach, our hobby will remain as strong and popular as ever, in spite of high prices and generally unstable conditions.

Variegated
yellow green
hen

Three parts
dark green

Self green
yellow hen

Clear white
buff hen

Self yellow
green cock

Self cinnamon
yellow hen

CHAPTER 10

How Colour is Produced

PLUMAGE PIGMENTATION

Colour of plumage in a canary is due to the presence of colouring matters or pigments that are carried to the feathers by the blood-stream. In the wild canary and the normal domesticated canary there are three colours: yellow, black and brown. Each is produced by a specific gene and transmitted as a separate hereditary unit.

Yellow is due to yellow lipochrome, which is of an oily nature and consequently tends to be spread more or less evenly through the plumage. In the canary, yellow is found only as a ground colour, that is the lighter colour on which, when present, the two dark colours of black and brown are superimposed in the form of variegation.

In a **Buff** the feather is thicker. The yellow colouring does not extend to the extreme edge of the feather; its edging is white, hence the bird's powdery appearance. In a Yellow, the feather is thinner and pigmentation extends to the extreme edge of the feather; a Yellow is rich and deeper in colour than a Buff.

One Yellow-factor can produce as rich and deep a Yellow as two Yellow-factors. Length or shortness of feather are not characteristics dependent on buffness or yellowness.

Whether a Canary be a Yellow Brown or a White Brown, the variegation it carries is due to the two colours of black and brown together or the brown alone. At present in the canary no other colour appears in the form of variegation.

The **melanin** carried by a canary affects its eye colour. When both black and brown melanins are present, a canary is dark-eyed. All birds carrying black have black eyes. When only brown melanin is present, a canary is pink-eyed.

A Yellow-ground bird carrying both melanins is dark-eyed and its variegation, if any, will be **Green**, owing to the effect produced by the black and brown when superimposed upon a Yellow-ground.

When a Yellow-ground bird carries brown, it is pink-eyed and its variegation will be Cinnamon, owing to the effect produced by the

99

single brown pigment when superimposed upon a Yellow-ground.

White Canaries are equal in type to the best Normals (Buffs and Yellows) in the various varieties. The breeder of Whites should pair White to Normal; from the former he obtains his colour and from the latter his improvement in type.

The better the Normal bird, the better the breeder's prospects. Quicker results will be had by using a Normal cock rather than a Normal hen as the cock can be run with two White hens for, say, a couple of seasons, by which time the cock should have paid for itself.

Of the young obtained from the first season, the breeder should pick only the best of the Whites. It is from these birds, which should show some of the desirable qualities of their father, that he must obtain his second season's Whites.

For this purpose a young White hen should be mated to a typical Normal cock, the object being to improve further the type of the resultant young.

The breeder may prefer to purchase a new Normal cock for these two young White hens, but if their father is in good condition this is not necessary. If it is a first-class bird, successful both at breeding and on the show bench, the wiser course would be to pair it to its daughters, which already carry the desirable factors inherited from their father.

This would, of course, be **in-breeding,** but the object of in-breeding is to obtain increased purity of one kind or another in one's stock. In this particular case, it is purity of type.

The **Recessive White** bird is homozygous (true breeding) for the Recessive White character. Mating two Recessive Whites must produce all Recessive White young. A bird bred from a Recessive White and a Normal Yellow makes a factor for Recessive Whites from one parent and the factor for Yellow from the other parent.

However, Yellow is dominant to Recessive White. The bird's plumage is not White but Yellow. By inter-breeding two such canaries to Yellow-factor birds, they would produce on average 25 per cent Normal Yellow young, 50 per cent Yellow-ground carrying Recessive White and 25 per cent Recessive White young.

A single factor for Dominant White suffices to produce a Dominant White Canary. However, a canary that receives two factors for Dominant White, one from each parent, cannot live. It dies in the egg or soon after hatching out. Thus the Dominant White factor is lethal in the double dose.

100

DISSIMILAR FACTORS

One point of interest should be noted by the novice; when a bird carries two dissimilar factors for alternate characters, such as a factor for Yellow and a factor for White, neither colour is affected by this association.

Yellow bred from a Dominant White is as pure in colour as one bred from two Normal Yellow birds, and a Recessive White bred from two Yellow birds carrying the Recessive White factor is as pure in colour and as pure for the White character as one bred from two Recessive Whites.

Some sample mating results are:

Dark-eyed White cock × dark-eyed Yellow hen gives White cocks, Yellow cocks, White hens and Yellow hens, all dark-eyed.

Dark-eyed Yellow cock × dark-eyed White hen results in White cocks, Yellow cocks, White hens and Yellow hens, all dark-eyed.

Dark-eyed White cock × pink-eyed Yellow hen give dark-eyed Yellow cocks carrying Cinnamon, dark-eyed White hens and dark-eyed Yellow hens.

Dark-eyed Yellow cock × pink-eyed White hen results in dark-eyed White cocks carrying Cinnamon, dark-eyed White hens and dark-eyed Yellow hens.

Some pairings for Blues are:

Blue cock × Green hen gives Blue cocks, Green cocks, Blue hens and Green hens.

Green cock × Blue hen results in Green hens.

Blue cock × Cinnamon hen gives Blue cocks carrying Cinnamon, Green cocks carrying Cinnamon, Blue hens and Green hens.

Cinnamon cock × Blue hen results in Blue cocks carrying Cinnamon, Green cocks carrying Cinnamon, Fawn hens and Cinnamon hens.

Some examples of pairing for Fawns are:

Fawn cock × Cinnamon hen gives Fawn cocks, Cinnamon cocks, Fawn hens and Cinnamon hens.

Cinnamon cock × Fawn hen results in Fawn cocks, Cinnamon cocks, Fawn hens and Cinnamon hens.

Fawn cock × Green hen gives Blue cocks carrying Cinnamon, Green cocks carrying Cinnamon, Fawn hens and Cinnamon hens.

Green cock carrying Cinnamon × Fawn hen results in Fawn cocks, Cinnamon cocks, Blue cocks carrying Cinnamon, Fawn hens, Cinnamon hens, Blue hens and Green hens.

10.1 A Green Border (taken from an old book).

GREENS AND WHITE BORDERS

Recently it has become apparent from reading the many show reports that at most open shows there was a marked increase in the number of entries of both Green and White Borders. A few words about these fine Border Fancy Canaries may create further interest in them and may give assistance and encouragement to breeders who are trying to build up a strain of their own.

GREEN BORDERS

Thirty years ago, the late R.J. Williams wrote that the ideal Self Green should be level in colour from the head to the end of the tail, with clearly defined markings, dark coloured beak, legs and feet, and the type, colour, position and quality as called for in the *standard* of excellence.

The desired colour is a deep, rich, grass green or what I would describe as a **holly green**, resulting in a bright yellow green with no smokiness or bonzy colour showing. The markings should be as dark and as clearly-defined as possible, fine and in straight, clear lines.

There are **Yellow Greens** and **Buff Greens.** The actual word Yellow can be something of a misnomer as there should be no suggestion of yellowness in either of these colours but the appearance of frosted evergreen trees.

Many of the best birds shown today sometimes fail in the colour of their legs and beak. These should be as near black as you can get them and it will be found that the purer and deeper the shade of green the greater the chance of getting dark legs and beak. Common failings in Greens are light throats and underparts, especially at the vent, bronze on the wing butts and near the thighs, and broad stubby markings.

Birds known to carry Cinnamon blood should not be used as they produce a shade of green which is too golden and often the cause of bronziness in the feather. Do not be alarmed at the brown markings on wing butts of young birds as these are usually lost at the first adult moult. Greens actually improve in colour up to the third year.

Breeding to improve colour

If the colour of your stock is getting too dull and smoky, introduce from the hen's side a good coloured Variegated Yellow from a known dark-eyed strain. This should brighten up the colour in the offspring.

This outcrossing should only be done when really necessary as it can lead to the light throat and underparts previously mentioned. The markings should not be too broad and heavy; the green ground must have a chance to show through.

103

If you breed a bird with very fine markings use it even if it fails in other respects. Yellow Greens have finer markings than Buffs and it is best to select for breeding, if possible, Yellow cocks with good markings. Giving away one point to gain another is, of course, necessary from time to time but this should be done with care and thought, always having in mind a bird of the ideal type.

Most of the best Greens retain the valued qualities such as correct movement, smartness of wing carriage and good quality, all of these being of primary importance. I hope all true lovers of the Green will treasure these qualities and not be tempted to lose them in return for size.

WHITE BORDERS

A really good White Border which is up on the leg, has a nice clean round back with a jaunty action on the perch and background feathers as white as freshly-fallen snow, will surely hold its own with any other colour of Border when the section special winners are selected.

I started breeding a few Whites six years ago and it has been very interesting each breeding season to see the improvement achieved in type while keeping the basic background colour pure white.

A weakness with some Whites is that in their flight feathers you can see a tinge of yellow. When selecting a White-ground canary from which to breed, irrespective of the variety, you should always pay particular attention to the colour and never breed from a White which shows any patches or tinges of discoloration.

When selecting a pair of birds to breed Whites, the two most important factors are type and, in the case of Normals, Variegated or Self (irrespective of whether they are Greens or Cinnamons), the background colour itself must be as true as possible.

If you wish to breed a good coloured Variegated or Self Blue, you must remember that the colour of the Blue youngsters will depend on the White bird's colour masking the Green in the bird you have selected to pair to it. In Whites there are Yellows and Buffs just as there are with Greens and Cinnamons. I always think that for a White Border to be able to compete for a best in section award, the quality of the feather is most important if advantage is to be taken of the White background colour.

When you are selecting a pair of birds to breed some young that will also be White-ground, one of the parent birds has to be a White or White-ground and its partner must be either a Yellow or Buff, Normal or Self in colour. If you are able to visit a fancier who breeds Whites, then do so. By carefully examining the shape and size of the white feathers you will be able to see the difference between the Yellows and the Buffs.

More Good White Borders on the Show Bench

There has been an increase in the number of White Borders exhibited at open shows and at All-Border shows. In three cases a White-ground bird was awarded second best Border in show. I believe that two of these birds could have taken the premier honours if their feathering had been slightly better in quality. If full advantage is to be taken of the White-ground Border's actual colour the feather itself should be neat, round and silky in appearance.

If, when selecting their pairs for the coming season, fanciers pay particular attention to the quality of the feather of the Normal bird and use a White-factor which has feathers the colour of freshly fallen snow, irrespective of whether it is a Yellow or a Buff, we can look forward to a White-ground Canary being best Border at a show.

One word of warning before making your final breeding selection: make sure that both the birds, the Normal and the White-ground, have type and a good back.

11.1 Nursery Cage — a useful item for the breeding season.

CHAPTER 11

Canary Management — January to December

The month of January is, of course, the start to the year and here is a month-by-month guide to just what should be done by the canary fancier.

JANUARY

This is the beginning of yet another breeding season and all breeders should concentrate on seeing that all his stock are in tip-top condition; it is a very important and very interesting time of year. If your birds have had a long busy show season, they should be housed in thoroughly disinfected flights or flight cages, with hens and cocks kept in separate cages. The birds should be fed a little softfood at least once a week, preferably twice a week; a varied supply of greenfood in moderation should be fed daily. I use, for example, watercress, sprout leaves, or cabbage leaves, but care should always be taken to ensure that it has been thoroughly washed in cold water. It is also advisable to provide daily feeding facilities. The staple seed diet to be fed should be canary and rape seed with a ratio of four to one with a little niger seed added. In the hens' flight there should be a supply of charcoal and this should be topped up twice a week; when scattered across the floor it keeps the birds active and interested in picking over the charcoal, when otherwise they would be sitting on the perch looking bored and not knowing what to do — birds are like human beings, they should always be kept active and interested. One thing I suggest that you *do not* do and that is to feed your canaries liberal amounts of antibiotics. All that is necessary is to feed a properly balanced diet of natural food. During the winter months of January, February and March I always give my stock all the cooked meat and chicken bones that are left-overs from the house; if we have had a chicken I break the carcass up into three pieces and give it in that form to the birds; at the end of a couple of days you will find that the bones have been polished, every little bit of meat has been taken from them; this is a very important source of protein for the birds during the winter.

FEBRUARY

Some breeders have started to pair up their birds at the end of this month using artificial heat to try and avoid the pitfalls of varying low temperature. To be on the safe side I do not recommend doing this unless you have seen just how an experienced fancier tackles the problem. Now a few words about diet: feed the hens as in January plus a condition seed once a week between each feed of softfood. You can feed the cocks condition food twice a week. Be sure to continue giving your hens charcoal, also continue giving all your stock a varied supply of greenfood and a daily bath in the mornings, not in the evenings when the bird will probably not have time to dry out before it goes to roost. For those who have hens sitting or laying, then you should reduce the amount of softfood to just a little given once a week, and no condition seed. The use of baths should be restricted to only a short period of time once a week. A little sulphate of iron put in the drinking water twice a week should be very helpful; the quantity is that equal to the size of half a dried pea.

MARCH

Early in the month the breeder will be watching with interest his birds coming into breeding condition; you should aim to bring your cocks into full breeding condition before your hens. There is nothing that brings a hen into her natural full breeding condition better than a strongly singing cock bird which is in full breeding condition. Continue with your February feeding and conditioning programme, increasing the amount of niger seed as given to your hens; if suitable greenfood at this period is in short supply then you should try giving your birds *sprouted* seed. If possible you should obtain young dandelion shoots or dig up the dandelion root itself and split it in half lengthways, and give it just as it is to the birds; the dandelion is nature's finest canary conditioner. When a hen is sitting give only half a teaspoon of softfood twice a week.

APRIL

By now each pair of your birds should either be busy sitting on eggs or, if paired up early, they should by now be feeding young ones in the nest. Keep the same diet as in March for the hens, but those that are feeding young in the nest will require sufficient amounts of softfood, etc, according to the number and size of young which they are feeding. If it has been your good fortune to have had several consecutive good breeding seasons, then you should not make any change to your recognised feeding methods. With the coming of warmer weather, all soft and greenfood tends to become stale more quickly, so all unused food should be removed from the birds' cage. If you are able to obtain chickweed that has *not* been sprayed with an insecticide then you should give it to your feeding hens, because to me it is nature's finest food on which to rear young canaries.

MAY

Follow the same procedure as in April; by now you should have some young ones feeding themselves and they should be in nursery cages. It is suggested that when a nest of young ones are old enough to be separated and taken away from their parents, a split ring should be put on their legs for record purposes as each one is removed. A nursery cage must be kept free of any stale or fouled food, and the cage bottom should be cleaned out daily.

When using perches for your young birds be sure to ensure (a) that they are made from *soft* wood and (b) that the diameter of the perches is small enough for the undeveloped feet of the young ones to grip adequately. As the young canaries reach the age of five weeks you should begin to train them to enter a show cage, as described in Chapter 2. In the case of Borders you should securely and firmly hang an old Border show cage on the front of the stock cage; a show cage should have perches in it made out of smooth or young growing twigs, with no spikes or anything on the twigs to damage the tender young feet. Before you hang it on the show cage, first drape over each perch a supply of chickweed full of seed or what other greenfood you have been feeding your birds on at the time. Always make a point of first putting in the cage a supply of the young birds' favourite greenfood, in other words, you train your young birds via the fondness of nice food, the idea being to gain their confidence in the cage on the very first time that the bird enters it.

With pairs of Borders that have young ones in the nest about fourteen days old, it is advisable to put a fresh clean nest pan complete with lining and a little nesting material at the other end of their cage; this should obviate feather-plucking.

A

B

11.2   Natural foods of benefit to canaries: A. Watercress.
B. Seeding chickweed.

JUNE

Your eldest young birds can now be put in a flight cage so that they can enjoy adequate exercise, but care should be taken to ensure that you do not put too many birds together in the same cage as this can be one of the reasons for them starting feather-plucking. If you can, obtain a nice soft sweet apple, cut it into segments and fix these firmly in the cage fronts, you will find that the birds will take to this very quickly, and it is not only easily digested by the young but it also aids their digestive system. Shallow baths should be given, during the morning only, to all your young birds which are in the flight cages. For those who breed colour-fed canaries now is the time to start your colour feeding. The feeding of the young birds and the old is to continue as in the month of May.

JULY

July is normally the last month of the breeding season; I personally do not believe in late breeding; this only means a late Autumn moult for both the young and the old birds. As soon as young adult hens complete their breeding season they should be put in flight cages, and you should continue to give them softfood and soaked seed twice a week to build up the birds' strength after a busy breeding season. The period before the moult is a very testing time for a bird's stamina. A shallow bath can be given every other morning. Do not forget to continue feeding well-washed greenfood right through the moulting period. By now you should be quietly handling the first round young birds in their show cages, but care should be taken never to frighten young birds. Always treat the bird carefully, lift the cage up by the bottom so that your hand is visible at all times to the bird's eye, and your movements are noted; provided that your movements are slow and careful the bird will not be disturbed in any way whatsoever. Above all, be careful to practise good hygiene with *all* your stock.

AUGUST

This is the most important month regarding the moulting period for your canaries. For the Border, remember that *no* artificial colouring stimulant or agent must be fed to the stock. For those of you who are able to obtain adequate supplies of green seeding dock there is no better form of seed to ensure that your birds moult out showing good natural colour with a nice finish on the surface of the feather. As the birds are constantly moulting their feathers and their droppings are loose due to their diet of softfood, soaked seed and greenfood, etc,

111

you should pay particular attention to the cleanliness of the cages and perches. To increase the birds' intake of protein you should give your canaries all kitchen surplus cooked meats, chopped and broken up chicken bones as you did during the winter months. Do not leave stale food of any kind in your cages. A little linseed can be given twice a week, it helps to give the birds' feathers a nice sheen. Be sure to stop feeding the hens charcoal until after the show season is over.

SEPTEMBER

This month brings the first birds through their moult and you should be able to start assessing these birds' possible potential. Now, while the birds enjoy clean fresh air, it must be remembered that no canary can remain fit and well if it is kept in a draught. Continue feeding a little linseed and plenty of green succulent seeding dock, shepherd's purse, plantain, etc, as they are all good not only for giving your birds that good natural feather colour, but they also assist our birds in their recovery from the strain which they have experienced during the moult. A segment of raw sweet apple should be pushed through the cage front, you will find that it is enjoyed by the birds as well as being beneficial to them and it will not stain their feathers.

OCTOBER

At least half of your birds by now will have completed their moult, and the rest will be on their way to doing so. Should one of your birds appear to have got stuck in the moult or is having a long and drawn out moult, an infusion of saffron (described in Chapter 2) should be given. The following treatment should put it right. Take a piece of saffron dried flower and then place it in a tea-cup and half fill the cup with boiling water. When the liquid has gone cold, empty the sick bird's drinker and pour the liquid from the cup. This should be repeated for four or five days. In nine cases out of ten you should see a considerable improvement in the condition of your birds. Continue to feed any seeding dock which is still available; although by now you will find that it is dry and has gone brown, the birds will still be able to extract some of the seed that is left and it will keep them occupied and reduce any possibility of feather plucking due to boredom in the birdroom. The use of baths can now be limited to twice a week but continue to give the bath only in the morning. You can continue feeding a little linseed mixed with your canary seed in the seed hopper. A small piece of sulphate of iron about half the size of a pea, can for the next month be put in each drinker once a week. This makes a good tonic for the birds and should be used as I said until the end of the month or the end of the show season, whichever comes first.

NOVEMBER

Birds which are in good health will finish their moulting in November and you will now stop feeding your stock softfood except the birds who have been out at the show. On the morning after you have brought the birds home from a show, a little softfood given to them can help them to recover from the strain of the show. Now is the time to scatter a little niger seed on the floor of the cages in the amount of a teaspoonful for every six birds; this I do primarily for my hens, it is not necessary for the cocks. It is recommended that all your show birds should, at this period, be kept in separate cages to avoid any disturbance to the birds' plumage. Continue giving a little sweet apple or boiled carrot, and also give a weekly morning bath. Now is the time to commence collecting your next year's breeding pairs, and if any new blood is required to breed from, introduce it into your stock now.

DECEMBER

The show season is now almost completed and all surplus stock should by now have been disposed of. The birds should have a quiet restful month and be fed on a plain diet of canary seed and rape seed in the ratio of four to one. I must make a point of continuing to feed them a little greenfood at least three or four times a week. For the next three months you should ensure that your birds are all kept active and interested in their surroundings — you do not want to go into your birdroom and look into your hens' flight cage and see them all sitting huddled up on the perch; they should be active either flying from perch to perch quietly or picking up on the floor of the cage. If you are fortunate enough, as I am, to be able to obtain a good supply of good clean wild seed from either a seed merchant or a farmer friend, then scatter a handful of this on the floor of the bird cages twice a week. It is amazing how it keeps the birds continuously active and interested in what they are doing. Continue feeding your hens additional protein in the form of cooked meat bones of all kinds; a little sulphate of iron in the drinking water once a week is also helpful, and I still advocate a weekly bath, in the morning.

113

12.1   Birdrooms.   Top: *the author's brick-built room.*
Bottom: *a typical home-made breeding room.*

CHAPTER 12

Tips for Border Fanciers

This hobby of ours is not just about breeding and exhibiting canaries; it is also about meeting other fanciers, making friends and sharing common interests. In this section I shall touch on several points which may interest Border breeders.

EXTRA VITAMINS

A topical tip for canary fanciers is to offer their birds rose-hip syrup. It is sold by chemists and health food stores and is rich in vitamin C. Added to the drinking water at the rate of one tablespoon to one pint of water, it is an easy way of giving the birds some extra vitamins during the winter. Provided in this way two or three times a week, it helps to keep birds in condition.

SWEATING CURE

There has been some correspondence in the past on the subject of 'sweating hens'. Although this expression is sometimes used, I would question whether in fact there is such a thing as a sweating hen. The words describe the state of some hens when they are rearing a brood, when their breast and stomach feathers become damp and matted in appearance.

This is not caused by the hen or the young sweating but by the young birds having diarrhoea. The excreta of normal, healthy young is sufficiently solid to enable the hen to keep the inside of the nest clean. This it does for the first seven or eight days by eating the excreta, as at that stage the food is only partly digested.

After the seventh day, food is fully digested by healthy young birds. They pass most of their excreta over the side of the nest, any remaining being thrown out by the hen. When diarrhoea sets in, the excreta becomes so thin and watery that the hen is unable to lift it out of the nest, which becomes damp as a result.

The heat of the hen's body draws the dampness into its feathers,

115

making the bird appear to be sweating, which is really not the case. Stop the tendency of diarrhoea in the young so that the excreta becomes normal and the sweating appearance of the hen will disappear.

One of the best remedies is to mix a little raw ground rice or raw arrowroot with the eggfood when given. To each teaspoonful of eggfood, add as much ground rice as will cover a one penny piece, or as much arrowroot as will cover a two penny piece. This usually has the effect of bringing things back to normal in a day or two. A pinch of maw seed given daily will also be beneficial.

LINSEED CONDITIONER

Linseed, if properly used, is invaluable in the birdroom.

It is very nourishing and is particularly useful during the moult, when it may be given fairly freely.

However, it seems that linseed contains a larger proportion of oily compounds than animals can easily assimilate, so it frequently happens that a portion passes through an animal in an undigested condition. When this occurs, the linseed is, of course, useless as a food, could possibly upset the digestive organs and might also act as a direct purgative.

This is particularly noticeable in the case of young birds. I have heard experienced fanciers express the opinion that it has been the direct cause of death because, in addition to the large quantity of oil, this seed also contains a high percentage of mucilaginous (gummy) matter.

Therefore, linseed should always be administered in comparatively small quantities and mixed with other seeds that are deficient in oily compounds, so as to maintain the balance between the two flesh-forming nutritional elements. One eminent fancier, who is a practical authority on bird feeding, states that during his birds' moult he always mixes linseed and canary seed in the proportion of 1 part linseed to 8 parts canary seed.

It has been stated on several occasions that canaries will eat linseed most freely during the early moulting season but some will not touch it at other periods of the year. If this were so, the instinct of the birds would seem to endorse the practice of giving linseed in its various forms for the prevention and cure of the troubles arising from adverse weather.

GENERAL CARE

Production of first-class birds depends on a clear conception of the Ideal and a sound judgment in the selection of breeding stock and in mating birds. Another important point is efficient housing, feeding and general management, including not placing birds in a draught or in direct brilliant sunlight.

Birds should always be given plenty of fresh air and suitable ventilation and not allowed to eat stale greenfood or stale softfood. Drinking vessels must be washed before being replenished. A cloth dipped in a little **non-toxic** disinfectant is admirable for wiping out the drinkers after they have been emptied first thing in the morning.

Fresh canary seed should not be added to seed hoppers until you have blown off the husks from the old seed. At least twice a week, empty the seed hoppers into a sieve to remove dust and husks and replace the seed in the hopper. It is advisable to give hemp seed not more than twice a week, with only a little amount being given at a time.

Canary seed should not be mixed with other seeds, except perhaps a little linseed during the moult; this will prevent wasted seed being scattered on the floor of the cage.

Cage floors should be covered with sawdust or some other removable matter and the cages cleaned out at least once a week. Birds' claws can be trimmed when necessary but be careful not to cut the vein that runs along the toe nails.

Fanciers are advised not to hurry when attending to their birds but to do everything as gently as possible without unnecessarily disturbing them. They should also be careful when removing a bath from a cage to close the door on which the bath was hanging (this is something on which I have slipped up only this past year).

A brick birdroom

With my brick-built birdroom, the birds have been, on average, about four weeks later reaching breeding condition than previously when a wooden house was used.

This is in spite of the fact that the brick birdroom, with double-glazed windows, never gets cold in the winter or as hot in summer as my wooden one used to do. I think the difference must be due to the birds' slow response to the little sunshine that reaches my birdroom.

Last year several of my adult birds, both cocks and hens, went into a very quick moult but, at the same time, were not lifeless. I fed the adults a little bread and milk one day and the next a little softfood to

117

which I had added a hardboiled egg. In addition, every day they had greenfood such as dandelion or watercress, both of which contain iron.

SPOTTING WINNERS

When you are trying to assess the quality of a Border, first and foremost look for type. It does not matter how good the quality of the feather is, or what a lovely long leg the bird has got because what we are looking for is the Ideal as depicted as our accepted outline drawing.

After type we look at the bird's head, which should be nice and round from all directions. The eyes should be in the centre of the head and the feet should be small and neat. To properly show off a good head the bird should have a nip in the neck or, to put it another way, a slight hollow where the neck joins the body.

For a bird to win its class today it is essential that it has a nice rise over the shoulders which, in turn, support and raise the flight feathers so that they should meet at the root of the tail and along the bottom of the back.

The chest should be nicely rounded, neither over prominent nor shallow. I like to see a long-legged bird showing a little thigh.

We must try to breed into our birds feather with a finish like silk, similar to that of a Long-tailed Grassfinch. Over the past six breeding seasons I have been trying to breed White Borders with this kind of feather, because if a White is to win a best in section award, the quality of feather is very important.

Looking back over 40 years of breeding Borders has made me appreciate the fact that there is no set feeding formula for success. The challenge and the uncertainty that meets every breeder each spring is something that keeps us in the hobby and creates the interest we all enjoy so much. But there are certain things you must do each spring if you are to breed any birds at all.

Caged separately

Your best birds should be caged separately. See that all show specimens are adequately trained before presenting them to a judge at an exhibition.

When handling birds see that you select hens which have a full, fleshy chest and long, nicely covered breast bones. The breast should slightly recede and be covered with a layer of fat.

Sometimes, a breeder has hens with which he does not like to part because of some good outward quality, although they are not completely physically fit. To use them for breeding is to cause disaster to their progeny.

Good qualities in hens, such as steadiness, cleanliness, sociability to the cock, strong maternal instinct, non-feather plucking, free breeding, and very good position, should be especially noted.

On the other hand, bad points, including timidity, hasty flying off the nest, uncleanliness, dirtying the food vessels, picking at eggs, mutilation of young birds, plucking etc, must be entered in the stock book.

Now, some advice about after-show care. Taking into account the fact that many thousands of canaries are exhibited, there will always be tales of sickness or even death. Firstly, make sure that your birds are completely well before entering them at a show; pay particular attention to any which had a slight setback during the moult: it may be wiser not to show them.

Immediately birds return from a show, if it is not too late at night, remove the show cages from the carrying case and scrutinise the exhibits. Any which appear out of sorts, fluffed out, or are inclined to sit humped up with ruffled feathers will need immediate attention. Position the cages in a **warm place** and give the birds water containing about four drops of whisky or brandy; a little sponge or plain cake with a few drops of sherry sprinkled on it is also excellent. Do **not give an ailing bird a bath**; warmth is called for.

Birds which return fit after a show enjoy a little of their regular softfood the next morning, or bread and milk sprinkled with maw seed. A fit specimen likes to bath and benefits from it.

13.1   *Some effective remedies which the Border fancier should keep.*

CHAPTER 13

Ailments and Corrective Treatment

Even the most expertly kept stock of canaries will, from time to time, develop some form of illness. On the continent of Europe canary fanciers have ready access to a large variety of antibiotics which they purchase from their local canary club. To me this seems wrong, as fanciers are giving their birds a wide range of drugs without any knowledge of either the correct dosage or side effects. I much prefer the British and Australian way of only veterinary surgeons controlling drugs.

SIGNS OF HEALTH AND SICKNESS

The body of a canary can give important indications as to its health. The breast should be plump and round but the breast bone should not be visible. A pointed, outstanding, breast bone indicates a defective system of feeding or the presence of disease.

The abdomen of a healthy cock should be flatter than the breast and a dark flesh colour. In the hen, it should be fuller and, when in breeding condition, rounded with a layer of fat which shows a lighter colour than the cock's. If a canary is out-of-sorts, place it on its back in the palm of your hand. Blowing on the feathers may reveal a brown spot on one or both sides of the abdomen just below the breast. Such spots indicate an infection of the liver and the bird should not be used for breeding.

When a canary is suffering from indigestion, even to the slightest degree, the feathers are not carried smoothly but appear fluffed out and are not as clean as those of a healthy specimen.

Imperfect action of the digestive organs is also indicated when a bird does not dehusk its chief foods — canary and rape seed — properly. Instead, it chews or grinds the seeds and bolts them down.

A condition often ensues just like 'going light'. As the symptoms become worse, the bird becomes fluffed up and tends to eat all of the time; as it grows weaker, it is unable to eat and so loses weight rapidly.

Likely causes are malnutrition or improper feeding; young put on to hard seed before their beaks are strong enough to crack it are particularly susceptible.

GOING LIGHT

This disease is self-explanatory by its very name; the bird gradually wastes away to a mere skeleton. To a newcomer to the fancy, birds when they first start to go light, actually appear to eat and drink more than is normal. This appears to happen much more frequently to nest feather birds than to adults. Birds with this complaint appear to have their feathers ruffled, and sit huddled in one position; they are usually between six and twelve weeks old.

The cause of the complaint is due mainly to incorrect feeding and lack of proper hygiene; never leave stale or surplus softfood in their cages. The thing to do is to make quite sure that you feed young canaries a properly balanced and easily digested diet. I personally never put young birds solely on hard seed until they have completed their moult.

PNEUMONIA

Canaries often suffer from pneumonia as they do not like being in a draught or very moist atmosphere. When a bird becomes ill, its body temperature immediately falls, so the very first thing to do is to put it in a warm hospital cage, which should be at a temperature of 25° to 30°C (77° to 86°F).

During the years that I have kept Borders, experience has shown that if a canary has a prolonged illness of three or four weeks, the bird's reproductive system will have been adversely affected, be it either a cock or a hen. I advise a little auramicin in the drinking water. Pneumonia may occur at any time of the year, but generally it is most prevalent in the spring when birds are coming into breeding condition; the other most probable time is the autumn.

INDIGESTION

Canaries do have indigestion and this is indicated when the bird vomits its food, causing it to be spread about the cage as it jerks its head. To treat the bird you should limit the amount of hard seed, and give it bread and milk with Maw seed sprinkled over it. If you add five drops of syrup of buckthorn to the drinking water the bird should soon be back to normal.

ASTHMA

Birds which have asthma have difficulty in breathing; it can often be the result of a neglected cold. Once a canary starts to breathe heavily it should receive attention. Give the bird a little egg food and bread and milk, and add a little glycerine to the drinking water. A bird which has a severe attack of asthma is best put down.

COLDS

A bird which is suffering from a cold will show this condition by sitting in a crouching position on the perch, with its feathers ruffled out, indicating a loss of body temperature. Immediately put it in a hospital cage, give it a little softfood, and five drops of glycerine in its water. After three days the bird should be back to normal.

BRONCHITIS

This complaint is shown by a bird coughing, sneezing, and wheezing due to congestion of the throat. This is often the result of a neglected cold. Again, put the bird in a hospital cage, give it some egg food and sprouted seed. Catch up the bird, open its beak and put down its throat three drops of *Terramycin Intramammary* solution twice daily — **Do not** feed bread and milk while giving this treatment. After only three days of this treatment you should see a distinct improvement in the bird.

FITS

You will sometimes have a bird which has a fit when handled, or if exposed to cold air. I do not know of a cure for this, so to keep your breeding stock vigorous and healthy, birds like this are best put down.

A GENERAL TONIC

For canaries which appear to be a little out of form I suggest that you make up the following tonic:
20 drops of glycerine, about 75 drops of tincture of gentian, 35 drops of tincture of quinine, two teaspoonfuls of lemon juice, mixed well together. Put five drops in the drinking water.

INJURED JOINTS

A very active and lively bird kept in a cage sometimes seems to get its legs and feet caught up in the wire front, resulting in an injured foot, joint or torn nails. You should catch up such a bird and soak the affected part in fairly warm water and **Dettol** disinfectant for a few minutes, then dry the wound and, with the aid of a tail feather, paint with tincture of myrrh three times a day.

SORE FEET

Birds which are troubled with sore feet can easily develop scales, which stops the bird from resting or even causes lameness. It is generally caused by allowing dirt or excreta to remain on the cage floor. This clogs the ball of the foot or nails. To rectify the trouble, soak the foot in warm water and **Dettol** and gently remove the dirt when it is soft. Dry the foot and paint it with iodine.

SCALY LEGS AND FEET

Some canaries develop ugly scaly legs; in these cases get a tin of zinc ointment and mix thoroughly with it a little paraffin oil until you have a soft paste. Then, using your first finger and thumb, rub the mixture well into the scales, twice a day. After a few weeks the scales will gradually fall off.

LOSS OF FEATHERS

This generally occurs at the back of the neck leaving bare skin. In these cases, catch up the bird, bend its head over your thumb and give it a thorough dusting with **Keatings' Powder**, obtainable from Boots the Chemists. With the bird still in your hand, work some Keatings into all its feathers with your fingers. A single treatment will kill off all the trouble — feather lice.

WARNING

When you are treating a sick canary, never give it even as much medicine as you would a child; a bird's body structure is so very much smaller that it is very easy to give them an overdose with fatal results.

CHAPTER 14

Feeding and Food Values

This particular subject can be split up into many different headings, but here are some suggestions which I have found to be most successful during almost 50 years that I have been breeding Border Canaries.

PREPARING SOAKED SEED

I like to use a mixture of seeds composed of: rape, niger, hemp, groats, making up 50 per cent of the mixture, and the remaining mixture to be teazle. This should be placed in a large jam jar and covered with hot water and left to soak for between 24 to 48 hours. Only fill the jar two-thirds full, as you will find that the teazle will at least double its size. Before giving it to your birds, place sufficient in a sieve and wash it thoroughly in running water. Be careful to shake out all trace of water before giving it to your birds.

Rinse the fully soaked seed, then spread it on a damp surface, such as hessian, and cover it over with a damp cloth; keep it in a warm place such as an airing cupboard for two days, and the seed will commence to sprout. When a seed commences to sprout its vitamin content and actual food value increases very considerably, and I like to feed it to my Borders twice a week during the winter, in addition to when the hen is feeding young birds in the nest.

POINTS TO REMEMBER

1. Keep all your seeds in a mouse-proof container in a cool, dry place.
2. Never use cheap inferior grades of any seed, always obtain your seed from a reliable seed merchant; remember you only buy a quality fresh seed at a fair price. Seeds that are in good condition are always clean, sweet-smelling, and are oily to the touch; you will never get the best results when using an old cheap seed.
3. Canary seed provides the birds with muscle building and warmth producing food.
4. Hemp seed used in moderation is beneficial to Canaries, especially for feeding hens when the young are ten days old; a little mixed with the canary and rape seed during the winter months is beneficial.
5. Linseed should be given in small amounts during the moult, as its oily content improves the quality of the feather, giving it an added sheen.

14.1 *Useful feeding equipment: multi-purpose plastic food or water container and clip on drinker.*

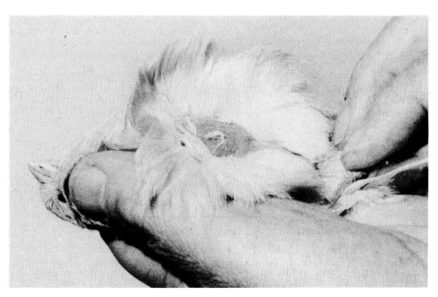

14.2 *The correct way to hold a canary for examination, to check condition, excess fat etc.*

6. Niger is another oily seed and can be very beneficial if fed a little several times a week to breeding hens during the winter months.

7. Rape is also a body-building seed and should be fed regularly throughout the year, and it will greatly assist in maintaining the condition of your stock.

8. Never take your stock or feeding methods for granted, always check the condition of every bird — the lack of this can be responsible for a poor breeding season or lack of success on the show bench.

9. Never leave your bulk supply of seed uncovered, keep it free from dust, etc.

10. Hygiene: cleanliness in everything in a birdroom is essential; pay particular attention to drinkers and all breeding equipment. The word 'hygiene' or lack of it will always be one at least of the reasons for any failure, be it during the breeding season or birds going out of condition at show time.

VALUE OF VITAMINS

Vitamin D can be manufactured by birds exposed to sunshine but this natural process cannot be depended upon even with stock housed in open flights.

Vitamin E (also fat-soluble) is essential to the health of stock kept in birdrooms and aviaries. Ordinary seed will not always provide for the birds' needs and so a supplement is often necessary.

Vitamin B is unlike the other vitamins already dealt with — they cannot be stored to any extent in the body and therefore require regular replenishment. Vitamin B consists of 15 components, each of which, while performing its own function, assists others in their work. It follows, therefore, that if there is a shortage of any one of the group the combined work of all the others will be impaired.

Vitamin C (the fat vitamin) is an important water-soluble kind. But because canaries can manufacture a supply in their own bodies, it need not normally concern the breeder.

Problems during the breeding season are many and varied but it is wise to remember that because the birds are under our control we must blame ourselves for at least some of the difficulties.

Clear eggs can be attributed to unfit cock birds, insecure perches, or feathers in the region of the vent which need clipping. A hen may desert the nest before hatching because of interference, infertile eggs, mice, or red mite.

A hen not sitting may be the result of lack of condition, lack of seclusion, or the presence of a strong singing cock. In the case of young hens, they may lay again in a few days' time.

Soft-shelled eggs are caused by a lack of calcium. Non-feeding hens may result from undue interference. If they are too busy watching intruders they cannot concentrate on their job; they sit tightly to protect their young. Some hens and cocks will feed only on certain foods, and you must provide those for them.

127

Plucking of young by parents is usually cured by placing them in a nursery cage, or partitioning them off with a wire slide. Chicks that pluck one another should be given a soft piece of string with which to play, and sprayed with anti-peck.

Young just out of the nest should not be given perches. And, when these are provided, they should not be smooth or placed too far apart. Always provide soft wood perches.

NUTRITIONAL NEEDS

Lack of data

The dearth of scientific data concerning the diet of cage birds has always been a handicap to breeders, not only in attaining show perfection but, to a greater extent, in combatting ailments that are directly attributable to malnutrition. It is different with other types of birds. Consider for example, the domestic fowl. It is of immense economic importance and, consequently, much money has been spent by government departments to find out as much as possible about its dietary needs.

Unfortunately, owners of canaries have had to acquire their knowledge the hard way. Although a commendable willingness is shown by all fanciers to share their experiences, this cannot be regarded as an adequate substitute for the mass of accurate data provided by research.

The following may be of help in this context:

Observations of experience

1. Carbohydrates. **A Canary requires fairly large amounts but because all seeds are rich in carbohydrates, there is little risk of deficiency.**

Fat. **Birds can convert carbohydrates into fat in their own bodies, and although seeds are normally poor sources of these nutrients, the possibility of a shortage is remote.**

2. Proteins **are of extreme importance to canaries. There is a real danger of deficiency in the staple diet, particularly with growing young and breeding birds whose requirements are greatly increased.**

3. Minerals. **A number of essential mineral salts, including calcium, phosphorus, manganese, iodine, iron, copper, and cobalt, are present in the usual seed mixtures but in insufficient amounts. The use of shell-grit and cuttlefish bone is only a partial solution, as neither contains all of the missing minerals.**

4. Vitamins A, B, C, D and E. **These are also to be considered when deciding on a basic diet for canaries. Mixed bird seed cannot be relied upon for the fat-soluble A and D vitamins. The former is necessary for growth, maintenance of health and resistance to infection. The latter is closely concerned with bone formation and the calcification of egg-shells.**

This is only a basic outline of the various foods required by canaries. Nevertheless, I hope that it will aid the discerning use of supplements.

The following summary may prove useful for reference as it also indicates alternative sources of the missing nutrients:

1. Animal and vegetable protein sources are eggs, milk, green-food and dried brewers' yeast. The safest minerals are those obtained from a veterinary surgeon or reliable pet shops. Among the best sources of Vitamins A and D are fish oils. Cod-liver oil can be mixed in with plain canary seed.

2. Dried brewer's yeast is one of the richest sources of Vitamin B. Wet yeast obtained from a brewery should on no account be used. Some green leaves contain certain components of the B group, but only in a low concentration. Pale green leaves, like those of lettuce, are of value in this respect.

3. Food deficiency is prevalent in young birds during the weaning period. Should they experience difficulty dehusking seed they invariably look for other food, such as a softfood mixture. They also drink a lot.

4. The treatment for 'going light' due to malnutrition is to give the birds liver extract and vitamins in their drinking water (some 15–20 drops per ounce daily).

For prevention in the young, I advise that it be added to the water which the old birds drink so that it is passed on to the offspring from the time they hatch until they are transferred to separate quarters. It should be continued right through the moult and until they mature.

Giving liver extract with vitamins throughout the breeding season avoids hens becoming finicky feeders, but the most important aspect is that stock birds are not depleted and, after the season has finished, they will go through their moult normally.

Liver extract with vitamins can be given to all of the stock throughout the year. The cost — a few pence a day — is amply rewarded by the decrease in losses of young and adult birds alike.

Bacterial infections usually prove fatal within a week, so birds must be treated promptly to effect a cure. Treatment is usually a broad spectrum antibiotic in the drinking water.

In America some canary fanciers grind up quantities of canary seed in coffee grinders and add it to their softfood as an added material form of protein.

ROCK SALT

Dairy farmers give their cows rock salt to lick. I recommend that in the winter months you provide small pieces of **wet** rock salt in your softfood dishes. You will be surprised how your Borders will remove the salty moisture.

CHICKEN PELLETS

Australian canary breeders grind up chicken starter pellets and add this to the normal softfood mixture, and I have seen some very healthy young Borders bred that way.

A1.1 Typical Australian canary room and flights.

Borders in Australia

CANARY ENTHUSIASTS

During my three-months visit to meet the many canary fanciers in the States of Victoria and Southern Australia, I called on breeders who kept Borders, Colour canaries, Norwich, Yorkshires, Glosters, Lizards and Crest-bred canaries, in that order of popularity. It was really an eye-opener to see the number of canaries being kept by a single fancier. I visited fanciers' establishments where there were anything between 200 and 500 canaries.

I noticed that where a fancier had a stock of between 300 and 500 canaries, he kept at least two and sometimes three different varieties. Even in these cases, where up to 100 pairs of birds would be used for breeding, all the young ones were close-ringed and a separate breeding record book was kept for each variety.

Having spent literally hundreds of hours talking canaries with Australian breeders, I would like to present some of their views. Those breeders who have looked after their birds during the moult and the show season, should soon be seeing their birds in peak condition.

Very often a novice with a good bird is tempted to over-show it, but it it has been properly fed and conditioned, this should not have too many ill-effects on the bird. In the opinion of Australian fanciers, birds which are well cared for throughout the year, do not need any last minute conditioning. This can often lead to clutches of clear eggs, dead-in-shell and bad feeding on the part of the parents during the following breeding season.

Some Australians give their birds softfood throughout the year and especially when they are returned to their cages the morning after a show. At the end of the show season they often give their birds softfood or mixed seed on alternative days, together with whatever greenfood is available.

If they find greenfood is hard to obtain, sprouted rape seed may be offered. Do not confuse this with soaked seed; sprouted seed is an invaluable addition to the bird's diet and can be given all the year round, especially during the breeding season.

All canary breeders in Australia keep their birds in exactly the same type of cages as we do here in Britain. They generally breed in single cages.

They use a variety of nest-pans, including one similar to our earthenware type but made of perforated aluminium sheet.

Although the temperature inside the Australian birdroom during the breeding season will often rise to 90–100°F (32–45°C) they do not experience any difficulty in eggs failing to hatch due to lack of humidity.

Needless to say the bird's staple food in Australia is locally grown. Canary seed costs much less than it does here. The average pay packet is two and a half times larger than ours, yet they complain about the high cost of seed!

Colour canary breeders use a completely different kind of nest-pan made of red plastic. It is about the shape and size of half a tennis ball. Strips of plastic are cut out of the sides and bottom.

At the back of the nest-pan are two plastic hooks enabling it to hang on to the cage front. The two hooks are made so that the nest stands well clear of the wire front which is not fouled by the youngsters' droppings.

Border canary breeders use a four-wire door on an otherwise standard show cage. They use shell grit on the floors of all show cages, not canary seed, although it is so cheap by our standards. The exception to this is the **Border Fancy Canary Club of Victoria**, which covers show cage floors with bran. This is because their show hall has a marvellously polished wooden floor and bran avoids risk of damage to the floor.

CLOSE-RINGED

All Australian canary fanciers close-ring their birds, as in Europe. The only major canary breeding country in the whole world where close-ringing of Border canaries is not compulsory is Britain.

During the past two years I have visited Border breeders in three continents, flying 30,000 miles, and it is my considered opinion that it is high time that we in Britain fell into line with the rest of the world by making close-ringing of young Borders an official requirement.

On the subject of Borders outside the United Kingdom, in all my travels I have not seen a single Border which could equal, let alone beat, the top British birds.

At shows in Australia, a small entry fee is charged. No class prize money or cash specials are paid out. Instead, clubs give some really splendid specials such as electrical appliances, cut glass and so forth.

The aim of the Australian Fancy is to award something that will give pleasure to the fancier's wife, not cash for the fancier's trouser pocket. There are also many handsome trophies which become the property of the winners.

LOWER COSTS

Booking the average show hall in Australia costs less than in Britain; that is, provided the shows are held in the suburbs. If a city centre hall is hired it can be very expensive indeed.

Most shows are one-day events. The **Border Fancy Canary Club** of **Victoria** event, which I had the pleasure of judging, was a two-day show. There were four stewards on duty all night.

Borders came in by aircraft from hundreds of miles away and some fanciers 600 miles by road — a good day's drive. Distance out there means nothing!

All Border fanciers were very keen to know how their birds compared with ours and with European birds. The average Australian Borders have very good feather quality but they are a little short in the leg and lacking in back or rise over the shoulder.

FOOD

There are three valuable foods neither imported nor grown in Australia; teazle, niger and hemp. As with us, the Australians use soaked seed in the breeding season. It consists chiefly of canary, broken sunflower seed, rape and millets. They feed it just as the seed starts to sprout and give it freely to their young birds until they have completed their nest-feather moult. Few Australian canary breeders supply many antibiotics — as, for instance, the Spanish do.

They make up all their own softfood, the typical ingredients of which are:

1 lb. (500g) arrowroot biscuits; 1 lb. (500g) **Quaker Oats**; one packet of **Farex**; 1 lb. (500g) wheat germ; 1 lb. (500g) bread-crumbs; one tablespoon Glucodin; one tablespoon of Trolax, a body-building formulation; one dessertspoon of **Aurofax D**, an antibiotic; a teaspoon of salt or crushed cuttlefish bone; and a tablespoon of powdered milk. One boiled egg is added for each 100 chicks.

The only moisture added is in grated carrot. When feeding this softfood to the hen they mix in one or two tablespoons of sunflower oil. No other liquid is added.   133

KEEN BREEDERS

I visited a very well-known and respected breeder of Colour and Lizard canaries whose birds would do well on our show benches. A great chap for improvisation, he uses round plastic containers for nest-pans and puts a felt lining in them.

He made seed-hoppers from plastic margarine containers complete with lids. He cut a ¾-inch hole out of the side for the birds to reach the seed. Very little seed is spilled.

He cut a piece, the size of a stock cage door, out of the side of a half-gallon (2.2l) soft drink container and suspended it from the cage front. It makes a very effective bath.

He showed me an Australian Canary nest-pan made about eighty-five years ago. Rounded, with a flat bottom, it was of cast iron. The thick green felt lining was glued into position. In those days this was the only type of nest-pan manufactured and nesting material was generally dried grasses and moss.

I was pleased at the large number of lady fanciers who readily participated in the all-important task of show secretary, just as Miss Wilkinson and Miss Mills do for the British Border Fancy Canary Club. Most canary clubs have lady exhibitors in their own right and I was pleased to see how many of their birds won specials.

The average Australian fancier builds his own aviaries and birdroom, generally three or four times the size of a typical British installation.

While in South Australia I met a Border fancier — John Horner; John, who is in his late twenties, lost his eyesight three years ago. Since then he has taught himself how to make a Border show cage; he has designed his own tools and jigs. One day I sat and saw him make a really excellent Border show cage.

Many birdrooms are planted with ferns and other greenery and some even contain goldfish ponds. Several fanciers I visited kept between 300 and 500 canaries. It was quite common for a fancier to make a round trip of 100 miles to attend his club meeting.

The average Australian fancier takes his hobby very seriously. With cities 600, and sometimes 2,000 miles apart I found there was a tendency for each State to have its own ideas of what constituted a good Border or how a Border should be judged.

I think that many Border breeders and judges in the States of Victoria and South Australia found food for thought after hearing how we in Britain select our breeding pairs and what we look for in a tip-top Border at major shows, where as many as 2,000 Borders might compete for the top award.

Out there, they appreciate that they have a shortage of up-and-coming younger judges, so they have now set up a judging school.

Practically all cage bird societies meet once a month. These societies are split into two groups — for budgerigars and all varieties of canaries. I found only one society which catered for all varieties of birds, including budgerigars, in each State.

The Border Canary Club of Victoria show received a record entry of 500 Borders which came from as far away as New South Wales, Queensland, South Australia and Tasmania.

The population of Australia is only twenty-five per cent that of Britain, so 500 Borders is equivalent to 2,000 or more in our country.

The birds were immaculately staged on stove-enamelled tubular frame staging with every cage placed end-to-end. The show hall floor was kept very clean, one steward being detailed to sweep up bran spilled out from the cages.

Awards are given only for the first, second and third birds in each class; so when I judged the novice classes, if I considered that the birds I would have placed fourth and fifth were really unlucky, I put a large red dot with a felt pen on the cage labels. If I saw a Border which looked like a very useful stock bird, but was not a show bird, I put a red tick on the cage label.

The novice section contained many birds that would have more than held their own at any Border show in Britain. On the Saturday, when the show was open to one and all, many exhibitors asked me questions about their birds, but I did not hear any complaints. How different from our shows here!

I had some 500 birds to handle so the whole of Friday was taken up judging. No one was allowed to smoke in the judging area, and stewards were not allowed to carry any of the exhibits by the handles at the top of the cage. They carried one in each hand, holding the cage at the bottom.

While a class was being judged, the next class was waiting on the table at the side of the judging bench. No one but the adjudicator was allowed behind the judging bench. No talking was allowed while a class was judged. In Australia, all canary fanciers keep rather a larger stock than we do, sometimes more than 500 birds.

To mark the end of our visit to Australia, on the night before our departure, a farewell dinner had been arranged unknown to us, by local canary clubs. It was attended by canary breeders of all varieties from as far away as New South Wales, South Australia, Tasmania and Victoria. We were very sorry indeed to have to be leaving so many genuine fancier friends.

A1.2   Framed diploma awarded by the Border Club of Victoria.

MALAYSIA

On my way home from Australia I had arranged to meet canary breeders in Kuala Lumpur, Malaysia. There I discovered that, although Malaysia has a population of some 14 million people, they had no canary clubs, only a society for native singing birds.

I had the pleasure of meeting a number of very enthusiastic Malaysian canary fanciers whose interests lay in several of the British canary breeds.

I have since put these enthusiasts in touch with English fanciers. The birds I saw had all been obtained from pet shops, and a mixed lot they were. I hope that by now a Malaysian Canary Club has been formed.

Borders in Spain

LECTURE TOUR

At the invitation of Señor Pulido, President of the Spanish National Cage Bird Show, I visited the event in Barcelona to give a lecture on Border canaries. The show was held in a very modern industrial exhibition hall. When I arrived, the president took me over to the Border section where there were three fanciers in attendance. There were no awards on any of the cages that I could see although judging had been completed.

I was asked to choose the three best Borders on show. In Spain they only select the best, second and third. There are no other awards. When I indicated my chosen order of merit, a senior Border official pointed to another bird and asked my opinion of it. I told him that it was, by British standards, a very poor Border. He then told me that it was the winning Border of the show and also his own bird. He then went to the bird which I had picked as best Border and said that this too was his. By the end of the show he told me that he had arranged to sell the supreme winner, but was keeping the bird which I had selected.

My lecture was given in a tiered horseshoe-shaped room. I had been asked to speak for one hour, but the questions and answers stretched it out to $2\frac{1}{2}$ hours. Afterwards, the president invited me to judge their show the following year.

There is no doubt that the Border Fancy is the world's most popular canary, not only on the show bench but in breeders' birdrooms. Canary breeding is immensely popular in Spain. The **Barcelona Canary Club** was founded in 1931 and today has a paid-up membership of well over 1,000 fanciers. The annual subscription of £3 is shortly to be increased.

They have their own club premises in the centre of the city. The front of the building which houses the club bears a big sign of a canary with the words 'Barcelona Canary Union.' The club is open seven nights a week.

AII.1   The entrance point to the Barcelona Canary Show.

AII.2   A Spanish all-wire flight cage.

Facilities include a bar and a games area for cards and so forth. There is a seed sale room, and the club also sells cages, linings, medicines and other aviary requirements.

As in the United Kingdom, the Spanish clubs have a very wide and varied programme of events at their meetings. These include lectures by experts, slide displays, film shows and up to 100 birds on display.

SEVEN-DAY SHOWS

Canary shows in Spain last for seven or eight days and fanciers go to a great deal of trouble to ensure that their birds remain fit and active for the whole of this period.

They use what they call anti-stress liquid in the birds' drinking water for three days prior to a show and two days after the bird is replaced in its stock cage. On the seventh day of the show I was amazed how very active and well all the canaries were in their show cages.

If a bird becomes ill during a show and goes soft, in the United Kingdom we put the bird cage in the warmth of the secretary's office. In Spain, it is given a medicinal tablet by the senior official or organiser.

The medicine is administered with an appliance which gently pushes the tablet down the bird's throat. I saw one bird treated like this at 9 p.m. one evening. The next morning I was delighted to see it healthy and very active on the perch. Needless to say that when I visited the club I purchased a supply of both the anti-stress and the tablets.

Also on the club premises, the president has his own office complete with desk and three easy chairs for visitors. The secretary has his own private office complete with filing system, and there is a lecture room with permanent staging for table shows.

There is only one type of show cage in Spain used for all canaries except Roller-type birds. It is a cross between a Gloster and budgerigar show cage with a budgerigar-type perch.

New Colours, Timbrados, Borders, Lizards, Glosters, Yorkshires and Norwich are all exhibited in this cage. The inside is painted white, the cage floor is covered with ground chalk. That is a regulation. The cages in which birds are exhibited and judged are supplied by the show promoting society.

During my lecture, I showed a new Border Dewar show cage, complete with a bird. They were extremely interested to see how

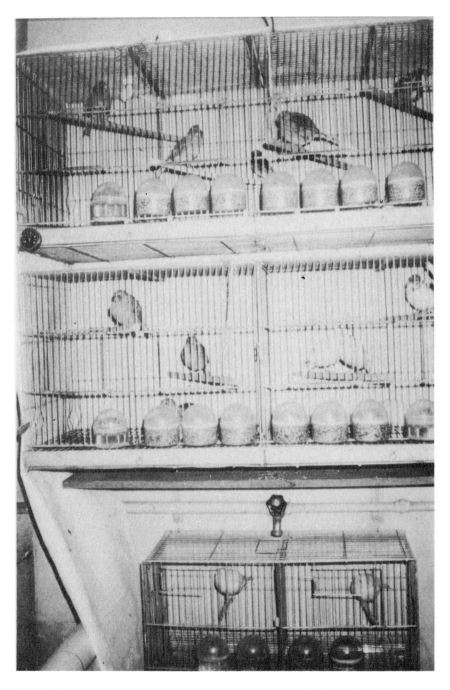

AII.3   Section in a typical Spanish balcony birdroom with all-wire breeding cages.

much more effectively one could see and judge a bird in a Dewar-type cage, and are actively considering using them.

The seven days of a major Spanish show are allocated as follows: one full day is for reception. This is followed by two judging days. The show is then open four days for the membership and public to view the birds.

Spanish judges follow the British *standard* of excellence for Type canaries. A points score card is made out for every bird. An exhibitor is given separate score sheets for each of his birds.

HONORARY OFFICIALS

Although the Barcelona Canary Union has all the paperwork associated with 1,000 members, no official receives any sort of honorarium, not even a box of cigarettes. They all work solely for the good of the club and its members.

For instance, the secretary produces and edits a thirty-six page quarterly bulletin with articles on canaries, advertisements and colour covers. It is mailed to all 1,000 members. The secretary receives no reward except the satisfaction of the task.

At the Spanish National Show some 3,000 canaries were on display, but I could see no indication of selling prices in the catalogue. The buying and selling takes place at the club table shows after birds have been judged.

Before a bird can be entered for a table show its ring number is checked to ensure that the exhibitor is the actual breeder.

There are far more canary keepers in Spain than in the United Kingdom, but unlike some British fanciers, no one thinks about making money out of keeping birds. When I mentioned British fanciers selling a single Border canary for as much as £100, they thought it dishonest.

After talking to Spanish canary breeders I am in favour of all British Border canary breeders being compelled to close ring all their young birds. Then the unofficial dealers would disappear in a single season.

REDUCING MORTALITY

Prior to the breeding season, to reduce mortality in the young birds, Spanish breeders put antibiotics in the hens' softfood. This appears to reduce the number of cases of clear eggs, dead-in-shell and young birds dying during the first seven days or so.

I am convinced that the average British fancier does not pay enough attention to the use of antibiotics, especially before and during the breeding season. The attention of Spanish fanciers to this problem appears to pay golden dividends.

Devoted to birds

The Spanish are a nation of bird lovers. Very few dogs are to be seen and even fewer cats, but a singing canary hangs on the balcony of every other flat. More than nine out of ten of the people within 20 miles of central Barcelona are flat-dwellers. The birds on the balcony are normally in double-breeding cages, of the all-metal and galvanised open wire type.

FOOD

In Spain there are no seed merchants such as we know. Importers sell seed only to unions (cage bird societies). Barcelona, which has a population of more than 3,000,000, has just the one canary society.

When the hens are feeding their young, antibiotics are stopped as these are used only for pre-breeding care.

Breeders mostly make up their own softfood, using dried ground-up sponge cake, antibiotics, hard-boiled eggs, chopped raw carrots and vitamins A, D, E, K3, B and C.

No water is added to the softfood. The only greenfood fed to the breeding hens is lettuce.

I called on the club secretary at his home on the eighth floor of a block of flats. Answering the door, he said, 'Shall we go and see the birds?' At the same time he produced an additional key from his pocket. He used it to open the next door flat and in we went. He not only kept his birds there but had a very comfortable lounge in another room and used a third for showing his excellent cine films.

INDEX

A

Ailments, *see* Illnesses
Australia
  Standards of Excellence,6-7
  Breeding and management
    techniques,132-4

B

Bathing,19,111-2
  during moult,45,50
Beaks,8
Birdrooms,47,55
  Bill Chiltern's design,57
  brick-built,117
Blue Borders,16,101
Body shape,9
Breeding
  condition,62,108
  for colour,99,103
  and diet,41,64
  and exhibiting,80,89
  preparation,54,61
  problems,73
  season,107-111
  see also Genetics

C

Cages
  cleaning,107
  for breeding,68
  for showing,24,28,81
  in birdroom,47,118

Carriage of bird,27
Carrying case,24
Chiltern,Bill,57
Cinnamon Borders,15,16,99
Claw damage,59,83
Clear Borders,14,15
Clear eggs,127
Close feathering,7
Close ringing,132
Clubs,1
Colour,14,99
Colour feeding,16,25
Conditioning
  for show,18
  during moult,26,116
Cumberland Fancy,1

D

Diet
  and breeding,41,55,64,69-70,86
  and colour,25,111
  and moult,26,41,46,49
  and nutrition,128-9
  seasonal,53,107-9,111-113,117
  supplements,40,129
Drinkers
  at shows,95
  for show cage,24,81

E

Eggs,69,76
  repairing shells,81
Egg–binding,65,74

Egg–eating,74
Exhibiting,17,26,89
   after–show care,118
   and breeding,80,89
   and condition,50
   assessing potential,29,46,89,118
   preparation,46
   season,112-3
   staging,94
   training,22-5
Eyes,8

F

Fawn Borders,16,101
Feather plucking,78,109,111,128
Feeding, *see* Diet
Feet,10,124
Flight cage,111

G

Genetics,100
'Going light',83,122
Green Border,15,99,103
Greenfood,19,39-40

H

Handwashing,90
Hatching,70
Head,7
Heating,108
Housing,117

I

Illnesses
   asthma,123
   bronchitis,123
   colds,123
   fits,123
   'going light',83,122
   indications,121
   indigestion,121-2
   injury,123
Infertile eggs,76

L

Labels,95
Legs,10,124
Line breeding,84

M

Malaysia,135
Moulting
   and diet,26,41-2,46
   and fitness,49
   season,111-2
   'stuck in moult',22

N

Neck,8
Nesting,54
Nesting material,64,68

P

Pairing
   correct time,65,108
   selections,2,61
Perches,28,81,109,128
Plumage,2,10
   loss of feathers,124
   pigmentation,99
Position,17
Publicity for shows,96
Purchasing,87

R

Ringing,109

S

Seeds
   linseed conditioner,116
   soaking and sprouting,19,125
   types,31-8
Selfs,14,15
Selling birds,83
Size,11
Show schedule,96
Societies,89

INDEX

Soft shells,127
Spain, management of birds,137-42
Sweating hens,115
Standards of excellence
Australia,6,7,
British,2-4,7
USA and New Zealand,3,12

T

Tail,14
Tonics,123
Training for shows,22-5,81

V

Variegated Border,14,15
Vitamins,41,115,127

W

White Borders,16,100,104
Wings,9

Y

Yellow Borders,99
Young Birds,51